Conversations with Anorexics

CONVERSATIONS WITH ANOREXICS

A COMPASSIONATE AND HOPEFUL
JOURNEY THROUGH
THE THERAPEUTIC PROCESS

HILDE BRUCH

EDITED BY
Danita Czyzewski and Melanie A. Suhr

A JASON ARONSON BOOK

ROWMAN & LITTLEFIELD PUBLISHERS, INC.
Lanham • Boulder • New York • Toronto • Oxford

A JASON ARONSON BOOK

ROWMAN & LITTLEFIELD PUBLISHERS, INC.

Published in the United States of America
by Rowman & Littlefield Publishers, Inc.
A wholly owned subsidary of The Rowman & Littlefield Publishing Group, Inc.
4501 Forbes Boulevard, Suite 200, Lanham, Maryland 20706
www.rowmanlittlefield.com

PO Box 317
Oxford
OX2 9RU, UK

British Library Cataloguing in Publication Information Available

Library of Congress Cataloging-in-Publication Data

Library of Congress Catalog Card Number: 94-70808

ISBN: 1-56821-261-5 (paperback : alk. paper)

Printed in the United States of America

™
⊖ The paper used in this publication meets the minimum requirements of
American National Standard for Information Sciences—Permanence of Paper for
Printed Library Materials, ANSI/NISO Z39.48-1992.

Contents

Foreword

by Theodore Lidz, M.D.

Sterling Professor of Psychiatry, Emeritus, Yale University

I WRITE the foreword to this posthumous work of Hilde Bruch with both sorrow and pleasure—sorrow, because the world has lost a great teacher and a fine human being, and pleasure in knowing that her valuable contributions to the understanding and treatment of anorexia nervosa will live on in this fine book. One of psychiatry's great clinical investigators and teachers, Hilde Bruch not only had a profound influence on psychiatry and internal medicine, but she was also able to convey her knowledge to the nonprofessional through engagingly written books. She was blessed with what Nietzsche termed "the bestowing virtue." Her curiosity and perceptivity about human nature were so great that her wisdom about people and their difficulties overflowed and enlightened others. Dr. Bruch was best known for her work on eating disorders, opening new vistas in the understanding of obesity and anorexia nervosa, but she was also an authority on the treatment of schizophrenic conditions, and this knowledge and skill contributed to her success with anorexic patients.

Hilde Bruch was my friend. My wife, Dr. Ruth Lidz, and I feel honored that she regarded us as her very close friends. We first met at the Phipps Clinic in Baltimore, where Ruth and I were investigating the family backgrounds of schizophrenic patients, and Dr. Bruch was completing her study of the family frame of obese children. We thus shared an interest in the family environments in which patients grew up, a topic on which few (if any) other psychiatrists focused their attention prior to World War II. Over the years we remained close, personally and professionally, freely sharing our findings and ideas, to our mutual benefit.

Although severely handicapped during the last several years of her life by Parkinson's disease, Dr. Bruch would not let the immobility that ended her career as a therapist interfere with her teaching. Resident psychiatrists at the Baylor College of Medicine cherished her as a supervisor of psychotherapy and gladly visited her at home for guidance. Dr. Bruch remained intent on completing this volume, transmitting her increasingly feeble voice into her dictating machine before she was finally silenced by heart failure. When I spoke to her on the phone just a few days before she died, she let me know in a scarcely audible voice that she knew her end was near, "but," she said with pride, "I finished dictating the book before I went into the hospital." I do not think that this great woman could let herself die until she had finished conveying what she had to teach. Those of us who cherished Hilde Bruch are relieved that her full and fruitful life ended before her increasing infirmities became too burdensome to bear.

Hilde Bruch received her M.D. from the University of Freiburg in 1929, and then obtained physiological research training in Kiel and pediatric training in Leipzig. She was well launched on a career in pediatric physiology in her native Germany, but when Hitler came to power, she left almost immediately for England. She then spent a year in a London child guidance clinic before emigrating to the United States. She obtained a position at Babies Hospital at the Columbia-Presbyterian Medical Center in New York, where Professor Rustin MacIntosh, the chairman of the department, recognized her brilliance and soon asked her to establish a pediatric endocrine clinic. Whereas some clinical investigators become famous by discovering a new disease or syndrome (which is then named after them), Dr. Bruch first gained prominence in 1939 by eliminating a famous but puzzling syndrome. Froehlich's syndrome—severe obesity, small genitalia, and sluggish behavior in young boys—had been attributed to an unknown dysfunction of the pituitary gland. Dr. Bruch demonstrated that the boys were fat from overeating and lack of activity, and that their genitals were of normal size but simply appeared to be very small because pads of fat obscured them. The finding led to an epoch-making paper, "Obesity in Childhood: V: The Family Frame of Obese Children," written with Grace Touraine. In it Dr. Bruch related the child's obesity to the mother's reaction to an unwanted child, for whom she substituted food for love, keeping him close to her at home because of her fear that he would be injured playing with other children. The mother's behavior was usually related to her own deprived childhood and to the passivity of the child's father. The study was among the first to relate a psychiatric or physiological disorder to the family environment in which a person has grown up. These early studies of obesity were characteristic of the skepticism of established but unproven concepts that marked Dr. Bruch's entire career.

In 1941 her recognition of the importance of emotional and intrafamilial factors to the etiology and treatment of illnesses led Dr. Bruch to pursue psychiatric training. She started her residency under Dr. Adolf Meyer at the Henry Phipps Psychiatric Clinic at the Johns Hopkins Hospital in Baltimore. Dr. Meyer was not only the most distinguished American psychiatrist of the time but a pioneer in psychosomatic medicine; he was also one of the few psychiatrists who seriously considered that schizophrenic disorders could be the result of critical deviations in personality development and thus amenable to psychotherapy—an orientation shared by Dr. John Whitehorn, who succeeded him while Dr. Bruch was a resident. At Johns Hopkins, Dr. Bruch also worked with Dr. Leo Kanner in child psychiatry and studied several children whom he had described as "autistic"; she disagreed with some of Dr. Kanner's ideas about the origins of the condition, but the study of psychotic children was to remain a major interest for her.

During her residence in Baltimore, Dr. Bruch entered psychoanalytic training, with Dr. Frieda Fromm-Reichmann as her analyst. Dr. Fromm-Reichmann, also an emigré from Hitler's Germany, could understand very well the trauma Dr. Bruch had suffered in leaving her native land and in losing most of her family in the Holocaust. The Baltimore-Washington Institute's staff of eminent training analysts included Harry Stack Sullivan and Lewis Hill, as well as Dr. Fromm-Reichmann. These three doctors were among the few analysts in the world seriously interested in the analysis of schizophrenic patients. They explored ways of modifying psychoanalytic techniques to the needs of these individuals. Here Dr. Bruch learned that psychotherapeutic work with schizophrenic patients could lead to insights into fundamental problems of human behavior not readily gained from neurotic patients. Here too she developed the perseverance that would be required to treat anorexic patients successfully. Her work with Dr. Fromm-Reichmann led to a lasting friendship that was professionally stimulating and personally rewarding to both of them.

Dr. Bruch returned to New York in 1943 to begin her own psychoanalytic practice. She became associated with the Columbia Psychoanalytic Institute and the children's service of the New York State Psychiatric Institute; she headed the latter from 1954 to 1956. Although she concentrated primarily on obesity and anorexia during these years, her interest in schizophrenic disorders remained undiminished as she interrelated it with her studies of weight disorders. She grew interested in the communication and thought disorders of patients in both areas, studied their family settings, and—collaborating with Dr. Stanley Polombo—came to recognize how parents' conceptions of their children's needs could lead to a child's misinterpretations and confusions of bodily sensations and physiological signals (such as hunger) as well as parental wishes. Dr. Bruch realized that the best intentions could miscarry, and she understood parents rather than blamed them.

Dr. Bruch also developed a major interest in fostering preventive medicine and psychiatry through educating nonprofessionals, a task for which her clear and concise style of writing was ideally suited. Her first venture into this realm was *Don't Be Afraid of Your Child: A Guide for Perplexed Parents*, published in 1952. In this book she sought to counter the confusions about child rearing that had resulted from the dogmatic advice provided by child analysts in the years following World War II—advice that was both contradictory and frightening, suggesting that lack of natural childbirth, cuddling, breastfeeding, proper bowel training, and so forth could permanently distort a child's personality. In contrast, Dr. Bruch held that parents' spontaneity and common sense in relating to a child are more important than many of the experts' very specific directives. Her next book for the general reader, *The Importance of Overweight* (1957), was also very well received and widely read.

In 1964 Dr. Bruch accepted Dr. Shervert Frazier's invitation to become professor of psychiatry at Baylor University. She arrived in Houston, in great contrast to her usual modest life style, in a Rolls Royce. "I was not," she told me, "going to kowtow to those Texas Cadillacs." The move proved very fortunate for this aging single woman. She soon felt at home in the warm, congenial atmosphere, and she found the young psychiatrists' eagerness for her supervision very stimulating.

Over the years Dr. Bruch learned a great deal about the personality characteristics and developmental problems that characterize patients suffering from anorexia nervosa. As this formerly rare disorder became common and reached almost epidemic proportions in young women, her familiarity with the condition enabled her to establish working relationships with patients who had been unwilling to begin treatment with others or to work at it meaningfully. She soon became known as the foremost authority in the field: she received referrals from all over the world and was besieged by countless letters seeking advice. She found herself in great demand as a lecturer, teacher, and contributor to scientific and popular journals. In an effort to disseminate her knowledge, she wrote *Eating Dis-*

orders: Obesity, Anorexia, and the Person Within (1973), which focused attention on the person within the distorted body crying to get out rather than on the manifest disorder. This extremely insightful and useful volume was followed in 1977 by *The Golden Cage,* aimed at the general reader, especially anorexic patients and their parents.

Conversations with Anorexics eloquently carries forth this tradition, allowing the reader to witness the therapeutic transactions between doctor and patient. I surmise that Dr. Bruch's determination to complete this book despite her serious incapacitation derived in part from a desire to counter the growing trend to treat anorexics by behavior therapy or family therapy alone, with little or no regard for the profound emotional disorders from which most of these patients suffer. Having had ample experience observing the "cures" obtained by such means and the continuing unhappiness of patients thus treated, Dr. Bruch emphasizes in *Conversations with Anorexics* the necessity of addressing these patients' long-standing and serious personality problems. Of course, she does not write about adolescents and young women who have been anorexic for a brief time or who may be participating in a fad or suffering temporarily through contagion from an acquaintance. She is concerned with patients who are profoundly underweight and have been resistant to various types of therapy. Indeed, Dr. Bruch does not neglect the impact of serious weight loss on emotional and intellectual functions. She believes that patients who are so markedly underweight cannot participate properly in psychotherapy and insists that such young women be hospitalized until they weigh at least 90 pounds before she will treat them on an ambulatory basis. They are often severely obsessive and their inability to recognize their life-threatening condition is almost delusional.

Dr. Bruch repeatedly draws attention to these patients' abysmal lack of self-esteem—its origins in the well-meaning but highly intrusive care given them by their parents—which a therapist must counter carefully but persistently. Most of these patients have felt it essential to please their parents and to support their parents' ambitions for them, even when these ambitions conflict with their own aspirations and needs. They are unable to express or even recognize the deep anger that their parents' demands, real or sometimes imagined, arouse within them. Dr. Bruch also shrewdly demonstrates the importance for both the patient and the parents (but at least for the patient) of recognizing the indirect and confusing communications from parents to which the patient has been habitually subjected. She vividly narrates how she manages to establish a useful rapport with these difficult patients through direct and open interest in their difficulties in living rather than by focusing merely on their dietary disturbance. She shows how responsive these patients can be to therapists who are interested in them as individuals rather than simply as interesting examples of a disease entity.

The inordinate value of *Conversations with Anorexics* to therapists, patients, and families lies in what the title of the book connotes—actual samplings of what transpires between a master therapist and her patients. The opening chapter describes the serious problems from which these patients suffer and the difficulties that therapists encounter and must seek to overcome; the remainder of the book provides clear-cut examples of how Dr. Bruch copes with them. The text gives the reader an unobstructed view of a patient's feelings of being an unwanted child despite—or because of—her parents' great concern for her, her efforts to deny her female gender and the bodily form that designates it, and the hopeless lack of self-esteem that leads patients to flirt with self-destruction—and some to achieve it.

Dr. Bruch led a full life, devoted to her profession, to her students, and, above all, to her patients. She was always engaged in solving the problems she encountered. She is gone now, but she has left a rich heritage that will continue to influence colleagues in both medicine and psychiatry as well as patients today and in future generations. Her colleagues have clearly appreciated her many contributions, for they have bestowed many prestigious awards upon her. Among these are the Joseph B. Goldberger Award in Clinical Nutrition, an award of the American Medical Association never before given to a psychiatrist, and—particularly gratifying to Dr. Bruch—a rare Golden Doctor (M.D.) special diploma from her alma mater, the University of Freiburg.

A dictated version of a book rarely can be printed as a publishable volume. Danita Czyzewski and Melanie Suhr have devotedly carried out the difficult task of transforming Dr. Bruch's manuscript into this significant book without the guidance of the author.

New Haven, Connecticut
September 1987

Conversations Remembered

A Former Patient and Her Mother Recall
Hilde Bruch's Impact on Their Lives

*The Patient: "She Gave Me Hope
for a Future"*

I FIRST met Dr. Bruch in the mid-1970s, when my parents and I traveled to Houston for a consultation with her. My situation was typical of those portrayed in this book: a teenager lost in the seemingly incomprehensible tangle of anorexia nervosa. When I was diagnosed two years earlier, I had never heard the term, and the illness remained largely mysterious to me in spite of my attempts at psychotherapy. The other physicians I had seen were only marginally helpful; they seemed as stymied by my distorted thinking and aberrant behavior as I was. In desperation, my parents wrote to Dr. Bruch, the recognized authority in the field and the one person who might provide guidance for us. We went to the consultation not knowing what to expect. I was hospitalized for medical treatment and subsequently was accepted for long-term therapy.

I came to my first meeting with Dr. Bruch young, frightened, and feeling hopeless. I was surprised at her age (older than I had anticipated), her style (articulate, gracious, and warm), and her calm command of the situation. Her authoritative presence was reassuring after the uncertainties of previous therapists. She was reserved, private, and methodical, but she could also have a sparkle in her eyes and excitement in her voice. It was this aspect of her humanness, her empathy and concern for her patients as individuals, that established the underpinnings of therapy.

Reading *Conversations with Anorexics*—and seeing much of my own life conveyed in these pages—has brought back memories of the other patients I knew and of Dr. Bruch's work with us. Her gift was a unique ability to communicate. She saved lives: not dramatically, but through the slow evolution of effective psychotherapy. Anorexia is a way of bringing order to one's universe, an attempt to freeze time and relationships. By gradually helping us understand ourselves, our world, and our illness, she helped us become individuals who could encounter the tasks of living and to venture, slowly and painstakingly, into the mainstream of life.

Dr. Bruch concentrated on the developmental origins of our illness and on fundamental aspects of self-identity rather than on the weight alone. Her approach was set forth in her original book, *Eating Disorders.* I read that book on our second day in Houston and was astounded: it described my situation, my confusions, and the answers I sought in my anorexic behavior.

For the first time, I felt I had found someone who could cast meaning on my life, interpret my behavior, and give me hope for a future.

Conversations with Anorexics beautifully illustrates Dr. Bruch's interactive method of therapy. "Active participation" was one of her favorite phrases. Her goal was for us to become active participants in life, but she applied the dictum to herself and the therapy sessions as well. This was quite different from other therapists, who would remain silent, presuming that patients should work toward their own solutions. I wrote in my diary: "She *knew* what she was talking about and would explain it or describe symptoms of other patients which were relevant to our conversation. She spoke with knowledge and sureness which no other doctor has ever had. . . . I could hear, accept, and recognize her analogies, though I was not able to express the concepts so succinctly myself."

Dr. Bruch provided guidance, consistency, and unflagging patience through the days and weeks of treatment. Therapy was not easy or rapid: gaining weight and at the same time exploring fears, motivations, and maturational issues buried under the years of anorexia was a formidable challenge. Yet she would not give up, nor would she allow us to. She was not uniformly successful: no one can be. Patients are as individual as their therapists and effective communication between the two is essential. Fortunately for me, she was the person to whom I could respond and who could touch my depths.

Dr. Bruch was guide, supporter, and counselor through our journey of discovery, of growth, and of change. She was professional and methodical. Yet with her patients, her humanness emerged. She knew each of us as individuals, each following a different path from emotional and verbal isolation to comprehension and acceptance of ourselves and our world. She walked ahead and with us; she was our leader and our companion, helping us reexperience the purpose and joy of life.

My last visit with Dr. Bruch was during a trip to Houston a year before her death. She had just learned she had cancer, and she knew her time was short and that the intervening months would be filled with fatiguing details of medical treatment and approaching death. Yet she continued to focus on her work for this book. Her attention was outward to the end: she spent much of her time compiling transcripts and case histories and a method of instruction for future readers. The publication of *Conversations with Anorexics* is a tribute to her: to her dignity, her eminence, and her dreams. I am honored to be able to say a final "thank you" to her. I also wish to thank her family, the physicians at the Baylor College of Medicine, editors Danita Czyzewski and Melanie Suhr, and the staff of Basic Books for enabling us—her friends, patients, and compatriots—to bring her last work to fruition.

The Mother: "Knowing Her Was a Great Personal Privilege"

Although I had few contacts with Dr. Bruch, I think of her not only with respect and gratitude but also with affection. She immediately impressed us, the parents, with her sure approach to the problems of anorexia, especially compared to the well-intentioned but fumbling efforts of other therapists.

We approached the first meeting with considerable nervousness and with my daughter protesting that there was no need to go to an "authority." Dr. Bruch was courteous and friendly but she was definitely in charge, outlining the steps we were to take: an interview with my husband and me alone, an interview with our daughter alone, and finally a meeting during which she would make recommendations.

My husband asked if she would accept our child as a patient, but Dr. Bruch answered that her days were too full already with teaching, writing, seeing patients, and consultations. She said that she would be able to suggest a course of action only after she saw the results of a complete physical examination, and after our daughter entered the hospital and stayed until she was no longer dominated by the symptoms of starvation. We followed this plan, convinced that if anything could be done, Dr. Bruch would be able to do it.

Weeks went by and our daughter suddenly appeared at home to pick up her clothes, announcing that she was transferring to a college in Houston, where she could continue under Dr. Bruch's care. We never learned why Dr. Bruch had taken her on as a patient, nor did we ask. We were only thankful.

In the following years, I appreciated the fact that she notified me every time she came to our city to speak, and I was invited to attend the lectures she gave to professional audiences. When my husband died, Dr. Bruch wrote a warm and perceptive note of sympathy.

When my daughter graduated from professional school, eight years after that first meeting, Dr. Bruch paid her the great compliment of inviting us for dinner at the Faculty Club as a celebration. Although her Parkinson's disease made it difficult for her to climb in and out of our small car, there was no diminution of her friendliness and warmth. I considered that dinner and her association with us, as a family, a great personal privilege.

September 1987

Editors' Preface

HILDE BRUCH had completed dictating *Conversations with Anorexics* when she died in late 1984. The manuscript contained a wealth of expository and clinical material illustrating Dr. Bruch's understanding of anorexia nervosa and the therapeutic technique that she had developed from her decades of experience with anorexic patients. However, because the manuscript was an early draft, Dr. Bruch had not yet had an opportunity to remove redundancies, to arrange the ideas in the optimal order, or to clarify transitions between ideas. As Dr. Bruch's workplace for twenty years, the Department of Psychiatry at the Baylor College of Medicine was eager to have her final manuscript readied for publication, and we were asked to assist in this process. Our interest in Dr. Bruch's work came not only from a professional admiration of her contributions but also from interest engendered by ongoing work in an eating disorders program (D.C.) and from having experienced Dr. Bruch as a teacher during residency training (M.A.S.). We therefore felt pleased and able to take on the editing responsibilities.

As editors, our task was to eliminate redundancies and to ensure a logical ordering of presentation of the text within each chapter. The expository and case materials illustrate specific issues in the dynamics and treatment of anorexia nervosa. We rearranged some of this material to illustrate chapter themes better and, in the longer cases, to present a developing picture of the patients themselves, the distortions of their experiences and perceptions that predated and accompanied the anorexia nervosa, and their eventual awareness and resolution of the underlying difficulties. Two patients, presented in several chapters, allow the reader to see how the same themes are manifest in different patients.

We made every attempt to maintain the style, the words, and, of course, the thought of Dr. Bruch. Frequently, however, we had to add transitional sentences and phrases to clarify the concepts presented, and we deleted a small amount of material from one case study because we judged it irrelevant to the theme of the book and because the rationale for inclusion was not available to us. In the remaining few instances when clarifications could not be made on the basis of either the rest of the book's content or our knowledge of Dr. Bruch's previous work, ideas were left as Dr. Bruch had dictated them.

We neither had nor sought access to Dr. Bruch's patient records. We knew that in past books, as well as in this one, she had disguised patients' identities by changing names and demographic characteristics, as well as by using composite cases. Therefore, to avoid the risk of unmasking already disguised cases, we made no attempts to change patient characteristics in the text.

The case studies in *Conversations with Anorexics* are much more detailed than those presented in Dr. Bruch's earlier work, especially those books aimed at nonprofessionals. In this book readers are given a rare glimpse of Dr. Bruch's style as she actively engages her patients in a therapeutic dialogue, an understanding dialogue that becomes central in the resolution of their anorexia. The details of the cases enable readers to appreciate more fully the characteristics of these young women who found a common solution to their problems in anorexia nervosa. While the themes of ineffectiveness, disturbances in body image, and misperceptions of feelings are common to all these patients, Dr. Bruch's final manuscript illustrates the transition from a sameness of presentation to the blossoming of many individual personalities in the course of psychotherapy.

DANITA CZYZEWSKI
MELANIE A. SUHR

Houston, Texas
August 1987

Conversations with Anorexics

CHAPTER 1

The Task of Psychotherapy

ANOREXIA NERVOSA as a clinical entity has been alive in medical thinking for more than one hundred years. Many efforts have been made to understand its occurrence and to find constructive ways to influence it. This book deals with my efforts to understand anorexia nervosa and the process of psychotherapy that I have evolved to help patients achieve a less painful way of living.

Anorexia nervosa is a puzzling and complex disease. Despite general agreement that many factors interact to bring about the overall condition, the range of unsolved questions about anorexia nervosa does not seem to diminish. For example, while once very rare, anorexia nervosa is now observed with increasing frequency. Once the original discovery of isolated tormented young women, it has now acquired a fashionable reputation, becoming something to be competitive about. It is not unusual to receive inquiries about young girls who express interest in "trying it" after they have been exposed to a movie on anorexia or if they have been involved in a science project in biology as part of their studies. This is a far cry from the anorexic of twenty years ago whose goal was to be unique, and suggests that social factors may have an impact on the prevalence of the disorder.

With increasing experience a new psychodynamic picture of the development of anorexia nervosa has been formulated. It is recognized that the underlying disturbances are much broader than traditional psychoanalytic thinking had assumed. (Originally the disease was seen as rooted in conflicts about sexuality and fear of oral impregnation.) Disturbances in self-concept and in the way experiences are perceived and conceptualized play a significant role in the disorder. While these patients suffer from severe dissatisfaction about themselves and their lives, they transfer this dissatisfaction to the body. The body is then treated like something foreign that needs to be protected against getting "fat," and this patients do through excessive discipline and overcontrol. Expressions of the deficiency in overall development are manifested by inaccuracy in perception and control of bodily sensations, confusion of emotional states, inaccuracy in language and concept development, and great fear of social disapproval. The relentless pursuit of thinness can be conceived of as an effort to camouflage these underlying problems.

In my early formulations, I recognized three features as characteristic of the anorexic illness: the nearly delusional misperception of the body (disturbed body image), confusion about body sensations, and an all-pervasive sense of ineffectiveness. Now I am inclined to visualize these under a more general heading, namely, as an expression of defective self-concept, the fear of inner emptiness or badness, as something to be concealed under all circumstances. Anorexics are extraordinarily successful in this concealment because they are over-compliant to the wishes of others. Perfectionistic behavior elicits approval from parents and teachers, who think of the potentially anorexic child as unusually good and competent. Some of the more serious conceptual disturbances can be traced to this pseudosuccess of being praised and recognized for fake good behavior. This praise reinforces the anorexic's fear of being spontaneous and natural, and interferes with her developing concepts, especially a vocabulary for her true feelings, or even the ability to identify feelings.

It seems that the façade of perfection and the praise for it is reassuring during childhood, often until adolescence. Yet this façade is not sufficient to ward off anxiety and panic when puberty and changes in social roles and expectations demand different behavior and coping mechanisms, for which these young women are completely unprepared. It is at this time that the preoccupation with the body and weight begins. The excessive ambition, the grandiose, completely unrealistic aspiration level that the parents expressed or the children read into their pride in them has now been internalized as representing their own goals.

The detailed histories reconstructed during the psycho-therapeutic inquiry reveal that many of the youngsters, some quite young, decided almost consciously never to show anything but behavior for which they were sure to get approval. Future anorexics are described as serious, precocious in their sense of responsibility, trustworthy, and capable of having adult conversations. For all these things, they are praised as being especially mature. When maintaining this façade becomes too strenuous, they finally protest and express their underlying frustration by giving up the behavior that they themselves call "fake." Having been overconforming and overcompliant, having acted as if they were more grown-up than they really were or felt, the reversal in behavior is so striking that it is rated entirely in negative terms, as hostile and deceitful.

Through work with many patients, I have been impressed that an anorexic's whole life is based on certain misconceptions that need to be exposed and corrected in therapy. Deep down, every anorexic is convinced that basically she is inadequate, low, mediocre, inferior, and despised by others. She lives in an imaginary world with an assumed reality where she feels that people around her—her family, her friends, and the world at large—look down on her with disapproving eyes, ready to pounce on her with criticism. The image of human behavior and interaction that an anorexic constructs in her apparently well-functioning home is one of surprising cynicism, pessimism, and bitterness. All her efforts, her striving for perfection and excessive thinness, are directed toward hiding the fatal flaw of her fundamental inadequacy.

Individual psychotherapy is only one aspect of the treatment needs of an anorexic. The state of starvation itself creates psychological problems that are more biologically, less psychodynamically, determined and that becloud the underlying issues. It is important to differentiate between the toxic state of severe starvation and the psychological preoccupation with excessive thinness. A certain nutritional restitution is necessary before psychotherapeutic exploration becomes possible and meaningful. This does not mean bringing the weight up to "normal." In my observations, patients usually start to function psychologically according to their personality, and not the state of starvation, when the weight reaches the range of 90 to 95 pounds, depending on the individual body build. When nutrition has reached that level, the psychological effects of starvation are less disturbing, and the acceptance of a more normal body weight becomes part of a patient's work toward self-acceptance.

Further, treatment of anorexic patients does not take place in an interpersonal vacuum. On the contrary, these youngsters are closely enmeshed with their parents and family. Superficially the relationship to the parents appears to be congenial; actually it is too close, with too much involvement, without necessary separation and individuation. This harmony, as it is described before the illness becomes manifest, is achieved through excessive conformity on the part of the child. After the illness has existed for some time, glaring hostility comes into the open. It is necessary to modify the family interaction. In patients younger than fifteen or sixteen, family therapy seems to be an effective way of resolving problems. However, family therapy is not a sufficient treatment after the illness has existed for any length of time or when the patient is old enough to leave home. In these cases, while the family needs to gain an understanding of its own role in the development of the anorexic child, the patient needs individual help to develop the tools for leading a self-respecting individual life with a capacity for enjoyment and self-directed identity.

Therapy involves the complex task of helping patients to break out of a closed circle of destructive thinking, experiences, and behavior. On principle, anorexic patients resist treatment and remain uncommitted to therapy for a long time. They do not complain about their condition; on the contrary, they glory in it. They are reluctant to let go of the "security" of their cadaverous existence. They feel they have found, in their extreme thinness, the perfect solution to all their problems, that it makes them feel better and helps them to attain the respect and admiration they have yearned for all their lives. Only reluctantly do they deal with the underlying erroneous assumptions that are the preconditions for this self-deceptive pseudosolution.

The therapeutic task is to help the anorexic patient in her search for autonomy and self-directed identity by evoking awareness of impulses, feelings, and needs that originate within herself. The therapeutic focus needs to be on her failure in self-experience, on her defective tools and concepts for organizing and expressing needs, and on her bewilderment when dealing with others. Therapy represents an attempt to repair the conceptual defects and distortions, the deep-seated sense of dissatisfaction and helplessness, and the conviction that her own self is empty and incomplete and that therefore she is condemned to compliance out of helplessness.

Therapy aims at liberating patients from the distorting influences of their early experiences and encourages them to look at their own development in more realistic terms. These patients need help with uncovering the errors of their convictions so that they can discover that they have substance and worth and do not need the strain and stress of a superstructure of artificial perfection. This is a difficult task, because the false reality with which they have lived represents their only way of having experiences, and patients will cling to the distorted concepts and will let go of them only slowly and reluctantly. In my treatment approach I directly focus on helping patients become aware of self-initiated feelings, thoughts, and behavior.

This book deals with the details of this therapy process, the ongoing exchanges between therapist and patient, and the awakening awareness in the patient of her own mental activity and psychological effectiveness. By calling the process "conversations with anorexics" I wish to imply that the patient herself needs to actively explore and understand what is going on within her. When I first started my work with anorexic patients, I found, quite by accident, that this active exploration led to improvement in the patient's psychological state. Initially I began to explore how the patient saw her development and her symptoms as a prelude to developing an alternative to traditional psychoanalytic treatment, which had apparently failed in being effective with anorexic patients. As it turned out, making the patient the significant explorer who was listened to, not only as a recounter of events but with encouragement to draw conclusions, represented the effective difference between the climate of experience during her early upbringing and the experience in therapy.

This book deals essentially with the individual psychotherapeutic aspects of treatment, and the title, *Conversations with Anorexics,* implies that understanding can be gained only by careful listening to what the patient has to say, rather than by speculations or attempts at fitting her problems into a definite theory. Unavoidably, as treatment progresses and experiences accumulate, certain common features among patients will be recognized. These common features may be aspects of the patients' individual development or of the techniques that prove helpful or hindering in the way the conversations are conducted. Because most of the patients I saw had been in previous psychiatric or psychoanalytic treatment, I devoted much effort to recognizing what had been useful or antitherapeutic in the previous approaches. In the development of my own concepts, I was guided directly by the patients' responses. Most, even those who came for consultation only, expressed in one form or another that the experience of being listened to and understood had been a great reassurance.

While the difference between the approach I describe and

current psychoanalytic practices is small, it was a distinct, nearly heretical deviation when first formulated during the 1950s. To me the amazing problem is that many patients seen during the later 1970s and early 1980s still are exposed to a passive type of psychoanalytic therapy. A college student who was seen by an analyst known for his work with anorexics stated, "He was cold and distant, never said anything except 'what it meant.' I did not feel that he understood me." She responded well to my comments that tuned in to the implied underlying difficulties; even during the consultation she accepted the need for her active participation in treatment.

Another patient reported in detail to the referring psychiatrist what she had learned during her consultation with me. The psychiatrist was impressed by the fact that she had truly listened to the issues that had been discussed with much directness in the consultation. This was in direct contrast to her previous responses in therapy. This young woman had been hospitalized twice for behavior modification programs. During both hospitalizations she had gained weight, which she promptly lost after discharge. Further, this patient had been nearly inarticulate in psychotherapy except for monotonous protests that talking about herself made her feel guilty and accused. During the consultation she felt that she was sharing in the experience. She felt she was able to "think out loud" about the idea that many of her symptoms served the purpose of perpetuating an "invalid style" that interfered with her living a normal life.

Psychotherapy with anorexics is difficult not only for the patient but for the therapist as well. Patients are difficult to work with in part because they deny that they are suffering from a serious illness and avow that they are unable to see the emaciation of their bodies or experience hunger when starving.

I feel that some of these treatment difficulties are related to the therapist's often unexamined suspicion that the patient's denial of illness indicates dishonesty. Therapists tend to deal with this dishonesty as if patients could change it through an act of will. For this reason, some therapists approach and evaluate anorexic patients in a critical manner, with a certain guardedness and prejudice, or even with open dislike. This judgment of dishonesty and deceit is often implied in the requests for consultation that I receive.

What is often overlooked is the fact that these young people have grown up under circumstances that discouraged honest and factual experiences. The usual assumption, by parents especially, is that the compliant phase expresses something good and desirable and that the changes when the weight loss begins indicate deception. However, it has been my observation that the undesirable features are the outcome of distorted early experiences. These distortions are readily apparent in the anorexic's handling of bodily needs, which have become organized in a confused and inaccurate way. Falsified hunger awareness and unreliable control over the eating function are the outcome of this inaccurate early learning and appear to be preconditions for the development of anorexia nervosa. Continuing this line of inquiry, it is also readily apparent to me that the so-called good or model phase in the later anorexic's life is the time when she experiences something that may be called systematic training in dishonesty. As a child she is praised and rewarded with approval for being "good" when she puts on a smiling and cheerful face. No attention is paid to the painful underlying misery, of which she too is scarcely aware.

Therapists do not need to agree with what they consider unrealistic—as a matter of fact, doing so would be dishonest; however, therapists must respect and accept, even if only temporarily, the patient's opinion and experience. A statement that she feels good, even elated, about weight loss may reflect what she actually feels, although it may be difficult for therapists to feel empathy. More likely they experience disbelief.

It is relatively easy to explain anorexics' misconception and misinterpretation of bodily sensations and experiences. Anorexics were not encouraged during childhood to be honest or accurate in verbal communication or in their view of the world. Instead, they were praised and encouraged to present an artificial front. Consistent with this early experience, patients describe their feelings of self, their bodies, and human relationships in honest though inaccurate ways. Therapists who have been unaware of the patients' early training and experience have focused on the "deceit" and unrealistic statements, rather than viewing the patients' communication as honestly reflecting their experience. A meaningful therapeutic relationship can be established only when therapists tune in on what patients express and experience. The anorexic patient can make important progress in finding a less painful way of living when a warm, human relationship develops between her and the therapist and when their verbal exchange has the openness and directness of ordinary conversation. Hence the title of the book: *Conversations with Anorexics.*

CHAPTER 2

Evaluation: Finding the Person in the Patient

THE OBSERVATIONS in this book are based on patients I have seen in psychotherapy or consultation since my book *Eating Disorders* was published (1973). In that period, over 500 patients or families initiated extensive correspondence with me, and I saw about 350 of these in consultation. While these patients come from a very broad geographic base, they represent the more difficult patients with anorexia nervosa, since they were referred for evaluation and, if possible, treatment after many years of illness and treatment efforts that had failed to bring improvement. This lack of improvement often included progressive weight loss as well as psychological deterioration while in the previous therapy. Demographically most of the patients for whom consultations were sought were females of adolescent age; very few were males, many fewer than the 5 to 10 percent incidence usually quoted in the literature. As time passed the age of the applicants increased, with forty-nine years as the highest at time of onset. Only a very few were still in early puberty.

Thousands of inquiries by telephone or letter came from all parts of the United States, and also from many different foreign countries, including Iran, Egypt, Australia, South Africa, Rhodesia, Turkey, France, Yugoslavia, Spain, and Ireland as well as many countries in Central and South America. Whenever possible, I made a referral to an experienced therapist closer to their home. Yet many insisted on coming to Houston for evaluation and/or treatment.

I worked out a certain routine in preparation for the consultation in an effort to see only those for whom consultation in Houston offered a reasonable chance of accomplishing something constructive. I requested a letter of referral from a physician and asked each parent to write how he or she had perceived the development of the sick child, the usefulness and disadvantages of previous treatment efforts, and what was expected from a consultation. The patients too were asked for a letter; without this there was the possibility—which occurred several times—that a patient would refuse to come after all arrangements for a consultation had been made. A patient's failure to comply with the request for a letter might express severe anxiety, negativism, or protest against being taken from one doctor to another.

After the preliminary screening through correspondence, the real evaluation took place, with the patient and her family coming to Houston. Parents or other significant people (increasingly often, husbands) were included in the consultation. Only in a few exceptional cases was a patient seen alone without relatives or friends. This situation usually reflected severe isolation and lack of human resources. Because of my cautious preliminary evaluation, I knew the "facts and figures" of the development of the illness, so that in my first contact with the patient and family I could focus on problems of living, the family and social circumstances, and other meaningful events that had precipitated the illness or had kept it going.

Many of these patients who had been sick for a considerable period of time and were in varying stages of malnutrition, needed evaluation from the organic as well as the psychological point of view. Quite often their nutrition was so poor that a meaningful psychological evaluation was not possible until the worst malnutrition had been corrected. For this, I prefer that patients be admitted to a *medical* service, with their weight gain supervised by an internist. (I try to avoid admitting patients to a psychiatric service, especially one where the primary treatment is a rigid behavior modification program to induce weight gain. Happily such programs are less common than they once were.)

I made a point of explaining to all patients the interaction between severe malnutrition and psychological reactions. Most of them had been harassed with threats to make them gain weight, just to achieve a "normal" figure. They and their families needed to be informed that there are two phases of weight loss; one is related to psychological considerations, which eventually need to be worked out in psychotherapy; the other is related to the malnutrition itself, which has a vicious self-perpetuating tendency. After a certain weight loss has been suffered, usually when the weight is below 90 or 100 pounds, an entirely new influence of malnutrition becomes apparent, namely, its interference with psychological functioning. A valid psychological evaluation cannot be done as long as the weight is at a dangerously low level. In my experience, most anorexics are capable of accepting this explanation and will cooperate, though to varying degrees, with a weight-gaining program to reach a nontoxic stage.

Not every consultation led to extensive treatment. Sometimes clarification of the often confused and contradictory procedures was helpful and facilitated future treatment. When the previous contact had been constructive, I advised the patient to return to the referring psychiatrist, who would receive an evaluation and suggestions for continued treatment. However, I often found—though less often now than even ten years ago—that anorexics' treatment needs cannot be met in their own community.

Whether or not I accepted a patient for long-term therapy depended on a number of circumstances: her willingness to maintain her weight at a nondangerous level; whether or not she was capable of maintaining herself in a new community, socially and workwise; and most important, her psychological readiness for introspective therapeutic work. Anorexic patients usually are convinced of the correctness of their reaction and behavior, and they feel rather strongly that they do not need to be in treatment at all, certainly not in psychotherapy. I feel that the patient must have some awareness of the denied or repressed pain, bewilderment, or despair that underlies the illness in order to become motivated to undergo the process of psychotherapy. If the patient describes everything as all right and complains of nothing, then there is no motivation or even capacity for change; without this, no improvement or recovery can take place. What she is willing to label as painful or bewildering, or as in need of change or clarification, varies enormously from patient to patient. Once patients openly express that there is pain and bewilderment, they and the therapist are on a much sounder basis for exploring the unknown and for stimulating effective changes. Attention to the patient's definition of her unpleasant experiences is important in order to gain an understanding of her overall attitude. It should be stated in the initial contact that therapy is conducted for the patient's sake, for her greater enjoyment of life (or however one formulates it), and not to fulfill parental demands.

Over the years I accepted about fifty patients for intensive psychotherapy in Houston. Therapy was on an ambulatory basis, with hospitalization, for relatively short periods, on a medical service if the condition demanded it. Some patients interrupted treatment prematurely, most often for external reasons, but also for difficulties inherent in the treatment situation. Others carried through until the underlying problems appeared to be resolved. The largest group who stayed for therapy were patients of college age who would live in a dormitory.

With the patients' and parents' consent, consultation or treatment sessions were tape recorded; much of the information offered in this book is based on these recordings. Many of the tapes, though by no means all, were transcribed. There are transcripts on more than ninety individuals, but the number of sessions transcribed for each varies greatly. In using the transcripts, the names and other identifying data have been changed. The information has been used for its content, to illustrate, in this chapter, how various anorexics described their view of underlying problems and, in later chapters, how this view gradually changes as treatment progresses.

Annette: "Simple" Self-Starvation

As illustration, I have selected for detailed discussion the case of a young woman who suffered from what I might call a simple case of primary anorexia. Her weight loss was due entirely to food restriction and hyperactivity; as far as I know, she never used vomiting, laxatives, or diuretics to accomplish a greater weight loss.

Annette was the youngest in a large family, eight years younger than her next older sister. She grew up in the capital of a western state where her father played a socially leading role. He had held high government positions until shortly before Annette was born, and he was now involved in banking and other business enterprises.

Annette had been a healthy child, and the pediatrician's records contained figures of her height and weight. Though she spoke of herself as having been "chubby" when ten years old, the figures indicate normal weight throughout. Menarche occurred at age thirteen, at a time of rapid growth in stature. The pediatrician noticed that her weight gain was somewhat low in comparison with her height. He explained it as probably related to the slender build of the whole family. Annette reached her highest weight, 106 pounds, at age fifteen, when she was five feet six and one-half inches tall. There was at first a slow and then a rapid decline in weight; upon graduation from high school her weight was 85 pounds, and it dropped to 70 pounds during her first year at a prestigious eastern college. She took a medical leave of absence, lived at home and attended a local college, and was in treatment with an internist and also a psychiatrist with whom, she said later, nothing meaningful was discussed. She gained some weight and returned to her college for the junior year. In some ways this year was more rewarding than the first year, when she had been homesick and isolated, but her weight again dropped to 70 pounds. It was at this time that a consultation was requested; she was by now twenty-two years old.

Several members of the family complied with the request for information about Annette, her early life and the development of the illness. They described the home as being almost ideal in its perfection; however, some family members mentioned that it was a place where it would be difficult for a young child to feel that she was a contributing member. One of her sisters expressed concern about Annette's ability to get emotionally involved in psychotherapy: "She could be interested in participating in a scientific approach—offering herself as a 'guinea pig' to some institution researching her illness."

Annette's own letter reflects an intellectual attitude: "I still have not been able to alter my attitude and approach to food and eating; I feel it is a struggle with which I alone must cope. . . . Closely tied with the problems of mealtimes are my fabrications or value judgments of types of food and the imposition of 'oughts' as to the amount I 'should' eat. . . . In trying to cope with the task of eating a balanced diet I have found myself most dependent on, and in rebellion against, my parents, most especially my mother. . . . I feel a failure and have a need to be in control . . . and I struggle with the problem of dependence and independence. . . . Outwardly I readily acknowledge that I am thin, tired, physically unattractive, and that I should gain some weight; but when it comes down to practical tasks, emotional reactions usually predominate."

Annette was in miserable condition. Her body was cadaverous and her face looked skeletal, with every bone showing. The border between cartilage and bone on her nose was clearly

19

visible. She admitted to being easily tired and cold (during July in Houston) and was unable to sit for any length of time. She was polite and friendly but restrained in everything she said, answering questions appropriately but volunteering little, indicating that she knew her weight was too low and that she was eager to gain weight.

This is an unusual admission. Characteristically anorexics will deny that they are too thin and refuse to gain weight. As it turned out, it was an expression of Annette's desire to give the "image" of being agreeable and cooperative. Three or four years later, after she had begun to resolve some of the basic issues of her anorexic condition, she vividly described the terrible stress and dilemma of that time: "I felt that I was at a complete dead end, that there was no future. We had tried everything [several medical consultations and attempts at psychiatry], and I felt trapped within myself and within the situation. The conditions that were perpetuating it were making it worse. There was absolutely nothing I could do or that I could see you could do to get myself out of this."

I reminded her later that the picture she presented at the initial consultation was nearly the opposite: "You were sweet and smiling and cooperative, promising you would do anything to gain weight, but nothing of the desperate feelings underneath came across." She explained that she couldn't possibly talk about it because it would have caused worry for her parents: "It was misery being caught this way and not understanding it, not knowing why and how. I didn't see a way I could ever get free of it. It's like being caught in the circumstances of almost a war, or a car accident, or something where all of a sudden you have no control and you don't know why all these ghastly things are happening. I had these feelings while still in school, and I think they are one of the reasons why I speak now of my fear of being alone, of feeling abandoned, sort of being like a helpless old woman, worn out, with nothing left. It is a projection of that same sensation and experience of despair. I didn't see anything to be gained by talking about how despairing I was, because I felt pretty helpless and hopeless."

Concern with the well-being of the parents, or efforts to protect them against any disagreeable news, is characteristic of the anorexic's attitude. It was particularly pronounced in Annette, and practically every memory she had contained this element. Currently too her thoughts and planning were deeply influenced by the question "How will it affect them?" In other activities that did not involve her parents, she was deeply troubled by the question of whether her interest was genuine or just an imitation of others.

To give one example: Annette joined a hiking group and became interested in birdwatching. She seemed to get great enjoyment from it, but at the same time she felt doubts as to whether she really wanted to do it and whether her enjoying it was genuine; she was unsure whether she herself considered it an enjoyable activity or whether she was participating only because the others were. Several years later she spoke of her real enjoyment of birdwatching; regardless of how it had started, she felt genuinely interested.

During the consultation Annette's parents expressed deep concern and great puzzlement about the changes in their formerly happy and well-performing daughter. They were worried about the role they might have played. As mentioned, Annette was the youngest child, and the mother felt that she had been the easiest of them all, including her grandchildren. She reported with pride and a certain amusement a scene of Annette's happy and trouble-free adjustment: She would obediently go for her nap; then she would wait patiently in her crib until somebody remembered her; she would never cry or ask to be picked up. When questioned about it, Annette said that she could not imagine, even now, that any child could have the audacity to inconvenience the grown-ups.

The family all agreed that Annette's childhood had been trouble-free, and they all remembered with amusement a scene from a formal Sunday dinner, where, Father felt, the worst things came out in children and he had to take action. Everybody remembered that once, though no one knew why, Annette was removed from the dinner table (probably during preschool days), picked up, and taken to her room. There was never a reason to repeat this; one demonstration of Father's power was sufficient and was silently accepted. There are no other memories of discord. Father mentioned that they always had dinner conversations on topics of general interest, not ordinary gossip or "women's stuff." He took pride in the fact that Annette took part in these discussions and was well informed on what was going on in the world.

Mother gradually became aware that Annette was trying too hard and was not rebellious like other teenagers, and she felt this was a problem. This was at the time of high school and campus unrest (in the late 1960s), and the parents reassured themselves that in many ways Annette's behavior was all right, that she was not like any of the troublesome teenagers who were using dope or becoming involved in sexual activities.

I explained to them, as I do in all cases, that the anorexia, the noneating, is a very late symptom in the overall development and that we were looking for earlier manifestations of oversubmissive behavior. Paradoxically the excellent, even superior, behavior about which parents speak with so much pride often is an indicator that a child was troubled, not only not self-assertive enough.

The mother confirmed my comment about Annette not having been sufficiently self-assertive. As an example, she mentioned Annette's submissive relationship to a friend of many years' standing who was unusually domineering. The mother was greatly relieved when this girl went to a different high school; she had felt helpless and did not know how to protect Annette against this influence.

After a week of evaluation, which included sessions with Annette as well as with her parents, the four of us met to discuss various treatment plans. We discussed whether the previous treatment program had a chance of succeeding. Annette and her parents agreed that it did not. An alternate question was whether she needed the facilities of a residential treatment center for long-term therapy. When we recognized that Annette was capable of being involved in psychological exploration, we gave up this plan. At this point, the parents left and Annette was admitted to the medical service for weight gain and further evaluation. There she made a good adjustment. Several other anorexic young women were on the service at that time, and she socialized with them and also with student nurses. She received an ample, well-balanced diet, and the trays left her room empty.

However, her weight increased slowly, more slowly than that of others who made a fuss about eating or not eating. The staff suspected that she might be disposing of food, but nothing changed when the bathroom was locked and the wastebasket examined for uneaten food. The other anorexic patients counseled her not to play tricks. Annette was sadly disappointed that even her friends mistrusted her. Much later she revealed that she had kept a diary in which she expressed more openly her anger about being suspected of cheating, but at the time she never brought these feelings into a session. Annette also explained how the suspicions and the extra supervision had kept her from gaining; if she were to gain now, that would prove that she had been cheating before—therefore, she restrained herself from eating more food. Her internist finally concluded that she needed more calories than had been offered at first. She left the medical service after three months weighing 87 pounds, not quite the goal of 90 pounds. She had enjoyed the hospital experience. She told how she had made many friends, not only among the anorexic patients but with other people as well, and some of these friendships proved to be lasting.

In her therapeutic sessions Annette was restrained in communication, but as her nutrition improved she became somewhat freer and more spontaneous. It is the therapist's task to help and encourage a patient to express what she feels, something for which Annette's early life experiences—and those of many other anorexics as well—had offered little encouragement. The session before her hospital discharge was more lively and spontaneous than any previous one, and also like many to come later on. She was pleased that she had been able to live on her own, in a new community and without any ties to her home. She said: "Well, I tried it and it worked. One positive thing was this situation's complete removal from everything that had gone before, so that everything was new and I wasn't doing it for any of the reasons I have done it before [namely, pleasing her parents and doing what was expected]. Mealtime was not associated with any of the previous thoughts which had dragged me down or had boxed me in. Now all options were open; there was no routine, no pattern to go before."

Annette also discussed her eating habits, how proud she would feel when she let her parents know that she needed to eat a lot to maintain good nutrition. The good news was that she could eat well and enjoy it. I closed the session on a note of caution, that with all the optimism and progress that had been made, she was still far from well: "The time here has opened up the fact that there are areas of development that have not taken place yet, and you need more work in that direction. Intensive therapy takes time, but it is necessary for your becoming capable of doing something which is of value to yourself."

Annette had decidedly benefited from the hospitalization, and a beginning had been made with psychotherapy. The plan for her was to return to college and to come for therapy after successfully completing the year. Her weight was now outside the danger zone, but there was no way of predicting whether she could maintain this while back in college.

With several other patients, similar arrangements were made; the onset of treatment was postponed until an important goal had been achieved, most often graduation from high school or college. This is advisable only when the patient is able to maintain her weight at a reasonable level and when the psychological problems center around developmental issues and have not been translated into depression or suicidal preoccupation.

Ida: A Reluctant Start

In Ida's case, the first contact was made by her mother, who phoned for an appointment on the suggestion of her internist. The mother expressed concern not only about Ida's low weight but also about changes in her behavior. She had always been a considerate, cooperative, and companionable girl, but now she had become defiant, irritable, and extremely secretive, and at times sneaky and openly dishonest. Ida had also become quite artificial in the way she talked and discussed things. She acted as if playing a role, not really taking part in living.

Ida had been an active and athletic child who had been considered unusually healthy. She had participated in the games and sports activities of her brother, who was six years older, and his friends. By age fourteen she had reached her adult height of five feet two inches and weighed 110 pounds. She had matured early, with menarche at age ten, and had regular menstruation until the weight loss began, at age sixteen. The picture was complicated by Ida's habit of taking laxatives, diuretics, and other medications "to help the weight loss along." There were no treatment facilities in her home state, and the chief question for the consultation was whether Ida could be in treatment while attending college or would need the facilities of a residential treatment center. At that time, she was nearly eighteen years old and would soon graduate from high school.

When Ida came for the consultation, accompanied by her mother, her face was nearly skeletal, with every muscle showing and contracting when she spoke or smiled. She spoke quite freely about the weight loss, which had begun on a trip to Europe two years earlier. First she had stayed with a family, as had been arranged by her mother, but then she decided to travel alone. She found that restaurants and museums were open at about the same hours, and she often skipped meals because she preferred going to a museum. She discovered that she could go for days without food and that it was "an interesting experience without great suffering." She was proud to have lost some weight, and after her return home she continued to eat very little. She also took laxatives, diuretics, and large amounts of thyroid medication, to the point of developing signs of hyperthyroidism. She increased her physical activities: swimming, running, tennis, and fencing. She slept less and less. There had been continuous efforts to make her eat more, but her weight was in the low seventies when she came for consultation.

Ida felt that being thin was what she wanted, and that there was nothing unusual about this. All the pressure to make her gain weight made her angry. She described her past life in glowing terms. She felt that her family had given her many advantages and privileges, and everything had been fine. The only unhappiness was her father's early and sudden death when she was twelve years old. But Ida felt she had no right to be unhappy, because she had everything she needed. As a matter of fact, she did not feel worthy of all she had received, and at times she was filled with remorse at not deserving such good fortune. She was puzzled that people seemed to like her and expressed so much concern about her; she herself felt there was nothing lovable and admirable about her. She was embarrassed now that her weight loss had resulted in so much fussing over her.

Before entering college Ida went on a cruise with her mother and felt quite guilty about all the luxuries on the ship. She compensated for this by exercising as much as possible. Though she felt miserable and cold, she would swim by the hour, and she lost some more weight. Despite her symptoms, she appeared so animated and actively interested in understanding herself that I felt she could benefit from psychotherapy while attending college.

I explained to her that her preoccupation with food and weight was an expression of underlying emotional and personality problems. Ida's treatment arrangements were made, which were to commence at the same time she began college, and she agreed to maintain and to improve her weight. She felt that she would be able to eat better once she was away from her mother's supervision and the continuous arguments about food. Ida was to fulfill her prediction, eating more than she had in a long time, and she gained five pounds within two weeks. She was so upset and shocked at this that she took large amounts of laxatives, diuretics, and whatever medication she had. When she came to her next session she looked hollow and extremely dehydrated, and she was taken to the emergency room where she was admitted to the medical service on an emergency basis. She had lost eight pounds and required intravenous electrolyte replacement. The internist explained to her that he could not safely discharge her unless her weight was 80 pounds. She was outraged when she heard that I agreed to this plan and said with much emotion, "Eighty pounds! Do you want me to hate myself?" In spite of her protest she cooperated with the plan.

Toni: Illness as a Way of Life

Consultation was requested when Toni was twenty years old, after seven years of anorexic illness. During that time she had become deeply involved in an invalid way of life and in arousing guilt and helplessness in the people responsible for her care. Toni had been hospitalized twice for lengthy periods and had also been in psychoanalytic therapy. Family therapy had been planned.

Toni was an only child and very close to her parents. She spoke in her letter of getting depressed when four years old, with "a lurking dread that something bad was going to happen." She hated going to school but began to like it in fourth grade. The onset of the illness coincided with the change to junior high school, something she had strongly resisted because she felt "like being pushed out of the nest." But she made a great effort to get good grades. In a class on nutrition the students were asked to keep track of everything they ate for three days. Toni did not want to be criticized and ate less than she usually did. After this she did not eat more than she had written down, because she wanted to be honest. Her weight went down very rapidly, from 110 pounds to 70 pounds. She had been prepubertal, but with the weight loss, signs of sexual maturity disappeared and she did not menstruate. At that time Toni also became less communicative and then quite withdrawn. Psychotherapy was arranged for but because she continued to lose weight, she was admitted to a child psychiatric service, where she felt quite comfortable. After her discharge she lost weight again and was admitted—against her lively protest—to an adolescent service, where she was treated with the brand-new behavior modification approach. The program involved restricting her to bed or to the unit lounge during the daytime. She developed the habit of staying awake all night, secretly eating huge amounts of food (which she later threw up), and staying in bed all day. She and her parents felt that the severe sleep disturbance from which she eventually suffered and the compulsive eating were directly related to this program.

After her return home, family therapy was instituted, but Toni felt that the therapist was against her, that he tried to force her into different behavior and activities. She made a serious suicide attempt that required extensive medical and surgical treatment, during which she gained weight. After discharge she worked hard to bring her weight down again by vomiting after eating.

During the first few sessions with me Toni was so anxious, hostile, and uncommunicative that I became as timid with her as her parents were. One of her often repeated accusations was that I made her feel guilty, that I put blame on her, and that this made her just more tense and anxious. Once I clearly recognized what was happening I raised the question of what she was doing to stop the grown-ups from functioning as they should. "Feeling accused" and "being *made* to feel guilty" became the focus of direct exploration. This question seemed to hit on an important spot, because she actively cooperated with this approach. I told her directly, in a supportive, not accusing, way that she did in fact feel guilty, not because I or anybody else *made* her feel this way, but because of the way she had conducted her life for the last six or seven years. I had noticed that she spoke of "feeling guilty" whenever something realistic about the future was discussed.

She had finished high school but had spent the last two or three years at hospitals or at home without any social life or regular activities. It could be shown to her that it was she who had deprived herself of many experiences that would have been constructive, exciting, and rewarding. I explained: "You feel guilty for not having pursued the promise of your own development. If you think of this now as accusing, I can only tell you it is not meant to be accusing and we would have to study why you understand well-meaning remarks in this way. I cannot do more than try to say it as simply and directly as possible."

After many objections, Toni was admitted to the medical service, and this turned out to be a positive experience for her. She summarized it in one sentence, that on the unit she learned that anorexics were not monsters (something she had felt during her previous hospitalizations) but nice people with whom she shared many interests. Her weight, on ordinary meals served in small portions, rose to over 90 pounds, which she accepted without complaint or guilt.

During our sessions we spent much time dealing with her fear of acting and behaving like a well person, somebody no longer handicapped by unmanageable symptoms. We also explored her refusal to cooperate with a sleep study. I explained that her behavior suggested that she feared there might not be anything wrong with her sleep and that it would all be revealed as a big hoax. She recognized that her threshold of feeling hurt and frustrated or discouraged was exceedingly low. This stopped her from even trying to see how anything new would work out. She also recognized that her continuous talk about enormous anxiety was related to her fear of not doing as well as she expected. She would get angry for giving up, and the anxiety she suffered was the reaction to her own anger. She finally agreed to a study in the sleep laboratory. To her amazement and relief, some abnormalities in her sleep patterns were discovered, and she received useful instruction on how to handle this. She felt relieved that she was vindicated, that it had not been an act, as people had been telling her.

On her return home, Toni reported to her therapist about what she had learned during the consultation, that she was less sick than she had presented herself, that she was ready to try a more normal life style. Toni felt it was extremely important that I had talked openly with her about her fearfulness and anger, and that she learned to "think out loud" while following my discussion. Toni returned from the consultation with a determination to examine practical possibilities of developing her talents in realistic terms, of moving away from her parents' home and attempting to be socially more involved with her peers. Treatment was resumed and it looked as if she was making genuine progress.

After several months a certain distortion in her sense of time became manifest; she felt caught between dread of the past and an equal dread of the past's repetition in the future. Toni saw no way to escape the perpetual repetition of events with which she had struggled. Although slow but important progress was made, her despair took over. About two years later she committed suicide.

Jan: The Shadow

Jan was eighteen years old when she was seen in consultation on request from her parents. The weight loss had begun two years earlier when she had been an exchange student in Europe. In the beginning of her illness she was seen by an experienced female analyst who died after a few months of treatment. She was then referred to a male therapist with whom she had little rapport; he considered her uncommunicative and recommended psychiatric hospitalization.

Jan was the second of three daughters. She had always been a small person; her highest weight had been 95 pounds. During the illness it had dropped to a low of 65 pounds. She finished high school but felt too weak to go to college, as she had always planned. For the past six months she had lived in her parents' home without any special activity, but she was overactive, felt depressed and bored. Repeatedly she would impulsively drive off in the car. She had had one serious accident, and her parents were terrified by the suicidal implications of her wild driving.

Jan came accompanied by her parents, and the consultation involved joint sessions, several individual sessions for Jan, and one for the parents. She was rather quiet during the first joint session. Unexpectedly, Jan was communicative when seen alone. She was eager to find out about the background and the meaning of her behavior. She felt that even before going abroad things had not been quite right. She had felt relatively happy as long as she "did not question things," did her work, and received good grades. Yet a feeling of no accomplishment had been gradually building up in her. She decided against going to college until she felt more secure about herself.

Outwardly this family offered the picture of functioning well and being trouble-free. They lived in a thriving midwestern town in which the father played an important role in the financial and cultural life. The older sister had always been "very emotional" and had demanded a great deal of the mother's attention. Even now when she was at college she would make frantic telephone calls to the mother. Jan had taken this older sister as a model, and she tried to be like her in every respect. Jan described her attempts to be "a shadow" of this older sister, but without making excessive demands on the mother. Practically everything she did was in imitation of the sister.

Jan had always been told that she was very mature, unselfish, and independent in comparison with this sister. But she felt that the illness was an expression of her own immaturity, that she was not pursuing her real life, that she had no goals and responsibilities. She was completely preoccupied with herself and her problems, and felt both depressed and discouraged. Now she was acutely unhappy that she had gone from the extreme of not eating to feeling that she could no longer control it. "Once I start eating I cannot stop—I go from one extreme to the other. It shows I'm compulsive in everything I do," she said. She had not developed any preferences but ate whatever food she found in the refrigerator.

In her individual sessions Jan was eager to explore why she had grown up without feeling adequate or capable of satisfaction. Even as a small child she never did things to please herself. Jan explained, "Basically I always did what my parents expected. All my life I have been trying to find out what I am supposed to be." Another time she said, "Maybe they should recognize my true self"—she was expressing a desire to be an individual but feeling unable to find out how to become one.

Jan felt that her sister got all of the mother's attention, the type of attention she herself wanted. But she felt convinced "that I could not develop my own self." She was aware that the anorexia was related to her inner insecurity: "I never got the feeling of personal attention and personal concern, and that has been building up over the years." I explained this aspect of the illness to her, that by reducing her body to childish proportions she had the power of a small child who gets overprotective attention: "But your true goal is the opposite, you want recognition as a mature individual and independent person who leads her own life."

Because the main point of the consultation was to evaluate whether ambulatory treatment was possible or whether she needed a residential setting, I asked Jan how a decision for residential treatment would affect her parents. She felt that they would have opposite reactions: Father would feel that because she was sick she needed to be sent away so that she could be fixed up and on return would behave like a normal young girl, outgoing and interested in men. Mother would see in the decision the confirmation of her own failure, that it would make public that she had raised a child incorrectly. Jan felt that her mother was the type of woman who was either a wife or a mother but had no personal life of her own.

In a summarizing session I reviewed Jan's main developmental points and symptoms. As to treatment, there were two alternative approaches. Treatment while she was at home would involve family therapy, which would lead to decisive changes in the ongoing interaction. This approach would probably be less time-consuming and also less expensive than a residential treatment center.

The parents returned home and within a month decided that Jan needed a residential setting where she could build up a reliable concept of an inner self. An important point in the decision was the fact that there was no psychiatrist in her hometown with whom she felt she could work and no experienced family therapist.

Jan and her parents kept in touch with me for several years. Jan made good progress at the residential center, became less rigid and inflexible, and left the center after three years. Several years later the father wrote to let me know how things were going. Jan had decided on a career in a semiartistic field and seemed to function well except for a certain social inhibition. She no longer acted or reacted in an "anorexic" way.

These examples illustrate the individual characteristics of anorexic patients and the need for an individualistic evaluation. Though these four patients appeared quite similar in their anorexic symptoms as well as in family and developmental considerations, they required different treatment programs. Two of the patients, Annette and Ida, entered intensive psychotherapy with me. I will present the course of their psychotherapy as the core material for this book, supplemented by brief references to other case histories.

CHAPTER 3

Consultation:
A Fresh Approach

A CONSULTATION is not a neutral experience, and more is involved than clarification of the underlying problems. Many patients are reluctant to come; some are seen in spite of their objections. Whether they come willingly or under protest, the fact that a consultation has been arranged conveys a definite feeling of hope that a new treatment approach may yet succeed.

The realistic need to attend to the anorexic patient's health can create special problems during psychotherapy. Some consultations are requested prior to the development of therapeutic and management problems, though most referrals are requests for evaluation of patients whose progress is unsatisfactory. Most of the consultation requests I receive come from psychiatrists who describe in details the difficulties they have encountered with a particular patient. Such a consultation requires an evaluation of both the interactional process between patient and therapist and an examination of the therapeutic relationship in the nexus of interactions with the patient's family and other associates. The referring psychiatrists have been trained at different times and in different "schools" of psychiatric and analytic thinking, but the problems they encounter show definite similarities. Usually the physicians focus on the abnormal eating and its symbolic significance instead of on the underlying developmental distortions and misconceptions. One approach that seems to perpetuate the anorexia instead of resolving it is the single-minded exploration of unconscious conflicts, oral dependency needs, and incorporation of cannibalistic fantasies in the search for fear of oral impregnation.

Another complication that can occur in the treatment of these patients is more difficult to correct. This problem arises when therapists permit the therapeutic relationship to become controlled by the patient's anxiety and threat of disintegration. Like an overanxious parent, these therapists perceive the patient as extremely fragile; by offering their "strength," a symbiotic relationship develops to which both doctor and patient may cling. Mistakenly believing that such support offers patients the chance to mature through the relationship, therapists become collaborators in maintaining the illness, sometimes condoning bizarre living arrangements and absurd eating rituals. Eventually therapists feel intimidated by these patients, fearing that continued visible signs of illness will expose them as inadequate. It is not uncommon for therapists to develop mistrust and at times open dislike for patients whose goal seems to be to make them appear ineffective, even useless.

The difficulty in consulting work is that patients whose treatment has come to a standstill may respond positively to the consultation and may see the problems in clearer and more insightful ways. But by the very nature of the consultative relationship, the patient will not be taken into treatment, and may leave with an exaggerated picture of "what might have been." Thus the consultant must explain during the consultation that this is an unusual procedure and that questions are raised or answered in a more precise and condensed way than would take place during ordinary treatment sessions. It is also important to allow enough time for a comprehensive consultation evaluation if possible. Not uncommonly a patient (and at times also the referring physician) expects that the evaluation work will be done within an hour, which of course is not sufficient to form a clear picture. In the preparation for a consultation, I explain that at least three or four hours scheduled closely together are recommended. At times as many as fifteen or twenty sessions over a two- or three-week period may be required.

Mira: Food Was Her Whole World

Mira, a forty-year-old married woman, had begun to be concerned with weight during adolescence. Before she got married in her thirties she severely restricted her food intake and lost weight, "to be more attractive." She also became amenorrheic. Her weight showed marked fluctuation, as high as 160 pounds and several times below 80 pounds. She alternated periods of severe dieting and enormous gorging. She tried to vomit but was unable to do so and therefore "suffered the consequences," namely, rapid weight gain when gorging, in spite of heavy use of laxatives. During the last starvation episode (with her weight down to 75 pounds) she was hospitalized and treated with behavior modification. She objected to this method and signed out after three weeks. Her weight continued at a low level for several months and then rose to around 120 pounds at the time of the consultation.

I received information about the course of her illness and difficulties through letters from the patient, her husband, and her psychotherapist, as well as through a hospital report. Mira described herself as the helpless victim of a compulsion; the husband was concerned whether her symptoms represented a real illness or were expressions of willful behavior. The therapist, with whom she had been in treatment for over two years, described her as a verbal person who, if allowed, would discuss nothing but her eating behavior. She had reacted with depression and anger to his attempts to make her face psychological issues. The question was whether she could be helped to deal with the underlying personality problems instead of ruminating about her eating behavior. I saw her eight times during a ten-day stay; her husband took part in two sessions.

During the first few sessions Mira behaved very much as her therapist had described, making her overeating and the way she did it the main topic; I accepted this as her way of presenting herself. She also gave detailed descriptions of various endocrine examinations, adding that she was resigned to not being able to have children. She had grown up as an only child in a well-to-do home, surrounded by adults who exposed her to the best opportunities in every field. She attended a boarding school in the East and then obtained a degree in business administration and had held several lucrative positions.

As a child she had a few, well-selected friends, and her

parents kept a close watch on whom she dated, worried that it might not be the "right type" of person. She recalled herself as having been a terribly good child, not allowed to "talk back" to her mother. She felt that the only way to assert herself had been though "not eating." Her mother had taken great pride in dressing her well. The mother herself was slim and well dressed—and still very much in the picture.

Mira met her future husband as a graduate student but postponed marriage for several years. She interrupted her own career and traveled with her husband, a consultant to several international firms. During these travels she suffered an intestinal infection. From then on she claimed "dysentery" as the cause of her frequent loose bowel movements, which in reality were caused by excessive laxative use.

Mira related her increasing absorption with food and dieting to a certain disappointment in her marriage: "When I was a child my mother always made things special, exciting, wonderful, glamorous—birthday parties, trips. I think I expected a lot of highs in my relationship with my husband and I wasn't finding them. No firecrackers, no rainbow, just ordinary living. I wanted the highs, the excitement. And I didn't find them, not in sex, not in life, not in anything—except I found them in food. Food makes me high, gives me glamour and gives me excitement, all the things I thought I wanted. When I am eating, I don't think about becoming heavy. I am completely absorbed in the glamour or the excitement of food. I only eat in restaurants that are very glamorous, chic, or very ethnic. It has to have some kind of exotic quality or must be gourmet, the best, the very best of this particular kind of food." Mira was pleased that she lived in a city with many ethnic and gourmet restaurants. She might go to several restaurants in a row during a binge. "I have to go to every restaurant and taste every kind of food. I don't have to eat the whole thing—I just have to taste it. I will go and order something, taste it and say I don't like it and send it back and get something else." Even when she ate at home she used only gourmet food from specialty shops.

During the first few sessions, Mira was so absorbed with her food stories that it was difficult to focus on other aspects of her life. At first she described her marriage as "excellent," but then admitted the difficulties. "I guess I expected the relationship to be the same as I had with my mother. Our marriage has revolved around my eating. When I eat and get fat, I isolate myself completely. Then I diet until I get thin, and then I can do things again. I can see people, I am right back in life."

Mira's husband handled the problems by disregarding them and staying involved in his work. For many years he believed that Mira's diarrhea was due to dysentery, and he seemed amazingly undisturbed when he learned about her laxative habit. He felt that in spite of some marital difficulties, affection and common interests had held them together. He was critical of the wide range of opinions that different physicians had expressed. While he had put his hopes on the recent hospitalization where behavior modification was used, Mira had resented the method. She explained, "I rebelled because I thought it was a violation of my rights as a person." When I asked "Was something achieved?" her husband answered with a certain satisfaction, "Yes, she gained ten pounds and was no longer in danger of her life." To this Mira responded with an air of triumph, "That's what you all thought—I never gained ten pounds. I cheated, and they were too dumb to find out."

After about four sessions, it looked as if an adequate picture of her eating habits had been obtained, and the purpose of the consultation was then to evaluate whether she might benefit from a change in psychotherapeutic approach. I began the next session with a statement along this line, that continued focusing on her food-related behavior would not contribute anything new, and if she really had not eaten for ten days, as she claimed, then that in itself would make the consultation meaningless. In order for me to obtain a meaningful picture, it was important for her to eat regularly. She responded, "Oh, but I was going to start with something else. I am so anxious and nervous today, and I know it is simply due to the fact that I started to eat yesterday. I had decided not to eat while I was here, but then my husband took me to a good restaurant and all of a sudden food became very important again. I had more salad dressing than I should have had, and I had butter. And now I am so terribly anxious and upset about it."

I responded matter-of-factly, "But that is the essence of why you continue to be ill, that you have made such completely trivial, irrelevant events the focus of your concern and thereby avoid dealing with basic problems of your life. Whether you have three or four spoonfuls of salad dressing is completely irrelevant." This she confirmed, but added, "You know, right now to me it is the whole world." I responded, "Right now the question is 'Can you achieve anything approaching a normal life as long as you focus on food as your whole world?' " She eagerly asked, "How can I stop doing it? I don't know how."

I reminded Mira how she had responded with glee to her husband's statement that she had gained ten pounds, and that she bragged that she had put on her heaviest robe, put coins in her pockets, and had not gone to the bathroom. "But you were more alive and natural and eager when you described how you had cheated them. That I would consider an important issue. I don't see how treatment can possibly be successful when 'cheating' is more important than fact-finding. I consider

42

the question of honesty and dishonesty a very relevant issue, a basic one. Our task here is to evaluate whether you can be simply honest and direct. This is much more important than what you allow yourself to eat. Our task is to evaluate whether you are capable or willing to pursue such an inquiry. Are you aware with how much pride you said that they were so dumb and had not noticed that you were cheating them?"

Mira admitted, "I have lied ever since I was a child." I elaborated on this: "The whole food business is self-deceit. There is nothing wrong with your organism so that you couldn't eat normally. So the whole thing is a lie. Let's talk about this, your reliance on lying." She explained, "Well, the reason I have lied has always been that I didn't want disapproval. I lie to avoid disapproval. The bad thing is that I was never caught. I was never found out and was never punished for lying."

I took up the implications of her remarks. "That's another way of avoiding issues: blaming it on others. You avoid dealing with you own role and responsibilities. Another problem is your tendency to make glib generalizations. This 'Oh, I did it in order to avoid disapproval' again avoids the real issue. We are here to examine whether you can benefit from psychotherapy, and for this the way you participate needs to change."

By this time she had become quite reflective and she spoke more slowly. "I don't want to lead this kind of life. It makes me very unhappy. I have led a very guilt-ridden life. I am constantly afraid of being found out, but maybe I am just basically immoral." I responded, "I doubt that you are basically immoral, but a requisite for psychotherapy is an honest effort to reevaluate what you are doing. The question is what you are willing to contribute to achieve a better understanding of yourself."

43

This may sound like a stern course of inquiry, and in a way it is. Yet I have found no other way of cutting through the obsessive ruminations, year in, year out, about upsets and nervousness in relation to food and weight, and to reach the underlying personal issues, the sense of inner emptiness, uncertainty and helplessness, and the lack of self-trust and self-confidence. Mira responded positively and began talking in an entirely different tone of voice. She spoke about her inner fears and uncertainties: "I behave as if I'm not worth anything. And yet I am not strong enough to—let's say—take my own life. But if somebody else would take it, it would be all right with me. Maybe that is too dramatic, because I don't really want to die, it is just that I am very careless with myself." She then described the long walks she would take by herself, late in the evening or at night, through deserted city streets.

Mira continued: "I also punish myself too much, force myself to do things that hurt me, but it is as if I have no alternative. Maybe it is because nobody ever punished me, so I have to punish myself now because I am the only one who knows how bad I have been and who will do it." I responded, "Let's find out more about what you call the bad person." She defined this in terms of her mother: "My mother has said to me often that she doesn't think that I am capable of giving anything to anybody." This I took up with "Let's talk about the inner doubts and the not knowing. I think that's where the illness begins, with the low self-esteem, self-condemnation and self-doubt."

Mira's past life experiences had left her with the conviction of being wrong—"not perfect." She related this to her early relationship to her mother, that she always had felt she was not as good as Mother. She had thought that this was the way it should be. "I couldn't be the way she was. Well, maybe I just never felt any sense of me." When I confirmed this as being exactly what we needed to talk about, she replied, "I never knew that I was supposed to be me. I didn't know how to be me." She had experienced feelings only through her mother: "It was through her that I experienced happiness, excitement, sadness—I never had an independent feeling. I have tried to substitute my husband for my mother as a person to share and feel the same feelings. I expected him to feel exactly the same way I do about everything, and when he doesn't I'm very disappointed. I need my feelings to be verified in order to know that I have them. I think I act as a mirror for what I think is expected of me under the circumstances. When I am supposed to weep, I weep."

None of this had been discussed in her previous treatment experiences; she had never talked on this level about herself. She added, "I don't think I ever really looked at my husband with the idea, 'I want to know who you are and I will respect who you are.' I always thought of him as just being my alter-ego, my support and extension, not as being a person in his own right." In further discussion, it became apparent that she had treated her therapist in the same way, as an extension of herself who was there to listen to what she produced but had no right of independent inquiry.

I summarized my observations: "What bothers me is that you are so aware of all this yet perpetuate it. Thus far I have missed any expression of intent toward change. I don't mean the food habit; I mean change toward your developing your own personality."

During the next few sessions, Mira opened up several new topics and "confessed" that she was afraid to be alone. She related this to her concept of time, that it is something to be gotten through: "It is like a thick forest, and when there are spaces I don't know how to get through and I get frightened. I live my life so that I don't have to deal with them." She recognized that this fear of empty time was related to her restlessness, "my inability to be at peace with myself, to be happy or content with my present state. I am very much afraid of these empty spaces, and it seems I cannot bear them anymore. I must learn how to fill time so I can no longer feel their emptiness."

The description of her fear of being alone and reactions associated with it were so vivid that I inquired how she had avoided bringing these problems up in her previous treatment. She claimed that her therapist had let her talk by the hour about food but had not helped her bring up any new problems. At times he had confronted her with her hostile feelings against her parents, which only made her angry and depressed. We summarized what had been learned during the consultation, that the food was not Mira's main problem; her failure at being a self-respecting, independent person who could be "good company" to herself was. This seemed to be related to her difficulties separating from her mother and her denial of the reality of other persons, including her therapist, as being separate from herself.

The question is, Why was this woman able to express her problems in a new way in such a short period of time? Of course, the events that precede the decision to come for a consultation play a role, as does the expectation that the expert will tell her what the problem is. To some degree this influences what a patient chooses to reveal during a consultation. I could tell Mira with authority that talking about food and behavior in relation to it would not solve her problem. No one had clarified that the development of her self and her attitude about herself and dependency on people were the issues rather than what she ate. During consultations it is important, however, not to hand down new formulations as insights of the consultant; rather, the patient should be helped to express herself, and her observations should be confirmed or examined for erroneous conclusions. The important thing is that the patient do the work and be reinforced in her honest self-discovery.

It appeared as if a great deal had been accomplished during the consultation. Instead of obsessively talking about eating and her upsets, Mira showed good ability to think in terms of personal relationships. The value of any consultation depends on how things are carried through. To me, the most satisfactory outcome is when the issues clarified during the consultation become the new line around which the work continues. Fortunately this is possible in many cases. Quite a number of patients took what transpired during the consultation sessions back to their therapists, or the therapists wrote for such information, and continued in a constructive way. In other cases, however, the value of a consultation is doubtful. Patients may experience a great stimulus in the intensive work of the consultation, but then may not find therapists with whom they feel comfortable. Mira was positively stimulated by the "discoveries" that were made. At the same time, however, the consultation aroused her anger or disappointment concerning the work with her previous therapists. She felt that the fact that we had discovered "something new" reflected unfavorably on the competence of her previous therapists, and she decided that therapy that did not focus on her special problems was useless. She therefore decided to try it on her own for a while.

Paula: Perfect Control

Referral for consultation usually deals with patients who have been in treatment for a long time and have not progressed adequately. Consultations are rarely requested for young anorexics or those who are in the beginning of their illness. Such referrals usually indicate limited local treatment facilities.

Paula was nearly fifteen and one-half years old when she was referred by her physician. She came from a medium-size town in one of the northwestern states, where her father and his brother ran a successful construction company. The physician felt helpless in stemming the progressive weight loss. The illness had begun one and a half years earlier with what looked like deliberate dieting; her weight dropped from a high of 107 pounds to below 70 pounds within that time. Paula proudly mentioned that she had lost forty pounds, had stopped menstruating, and had kept up a rigid, strenuous exercise program. She had been referred to a psychologist with whom she developed little rapport; and she had refused to see him again.

Detailed information was obtained during the first two sessions when Paula was seen together with her parents. She was the second daughter; her older sister walked with a limp, caused by a congenital malformation, and was quiet and socially rather shy. Paula herself was described as an outstanding child who was successful in everything she undertook. She was helpful at home and acted like a little mother toward a younger brother, for whom she would fix breakfast and whom she accompanied to school. Until she became anorexic, Paula had been valued as superior in performance, artistically gifted, helpful, neat and well dressed. The dieting began when she felt the need to be "more perfect." She had suffered a painful disappointment when no boy had asked her to go with him to attend a prom. To her, this was a public humiliation and made her feel ugly and undesirable.

In her introductory letter she wrote: "I was left without anyone to ask. This worried me awfully bad—I cried and cried over it until finally I asked this friend I knew from church but he said he had an out-of-town tournament that weekend. So I didn't go, and this really upset me because I was worried over what others would think. I decided I needed to lose a little weight. I wanted to be a perfect, slim model size. So I just cut down on what I ate. About the middle of the month I had my last good period. After I'd lost about five pounds I decided to keep it up—it wasn't that hard to lose weight—and besides, if I got under 'perfect' I could eat everything." She thought she would gain some weight during a vacation trip of the whole family. Instead: "I wouldn't or couldn't get myself to eat very much—so I lost more weight."

The next spring she suffered the same disappointment. "I was really busy in school and before I knew it, it was May. Now it was time to find somebody to go to the prom with. I felt someone surely would ask me. Sure enough, no one did. As I feared, I didn't go. It didn't really bother me that much, but one night each week I'd binge and eat one half-gallon of ice cream and would fast the next day."

At that time her physician provided her with a diet. "He and I were going to get me to the right size and keep me that way. 'Perfect control!' I am trying to get well, but I'm just scared to and I think I never will. I really hate myself for all this—just look what I have done to myself. I wish I could die and go to heaven and eat ice cream forever."

Paula was quiet during the joint session, but when I saw her alone she talked freely. "I'm scared that if I'm not a big shot I won't be respected." I encouraged her to express her feelings further: "You are scared that your parents don't help you enough. You see, this is a funny illness. It sounds as if it were an illness of appetite and food and weight, but it isn't. It is an illness of self-respect, of how one rates oneself in relation to others. You said that people who didn't go to the prom wouldn't be respected. Let's hear more about what it really means to you." With much reluctance and visible conflict of loyalty, Paula talked about her discontent with her family's social situation.

Paula's parents were desperate about the manner in which the illness had changed the whole atmosphere of the home, but they spoke with a certain detachment about some family problems. Father and his brother had a good working relationship in their business but little contact privately. Paula's father had met her mother during his training on the West Coast, and she had been reluctant to move to the smaller town where the family business was located. His brother had married a hometown girl, the daughter of the leading family, who now herself played an important role in the town's social life. Paula's mother was treated like an outsider, not really accepted by her in-laws, in particular not by her successful sister-in-law. Paula's parents in turn considered the other family too snobbish and concerned only with externals. With much emotion Paula asked, "Do you think it should be the way it is, or should it be the way my aunt does it? Well, I don't think it should be that way. I don't think ours is a good way either. All my friends, and all the other wives go along. I just want to be respected. I don't want to be thought of as a nobody."

I continued to encourage her to express herself freely, saying that this issue was important to her, though her parents made light of it. "That's why I wanted to talk with you alone. I realized you wouldn't talk when your parents were present." She became more outspoken and began to look angry: "I don't know if you will respect it or not, but I wish there was a way that I could be just me and be respected. I can't figure out why I'm on that diet. I seriously thought I was chunky before I went on the diet. But after I got down to being just right, I don't know why I kept on with the diet."

When Paula entered junior high school she felt that she was being snubbed and disregarded, and felt as if she did not belong. One of the troubles was that she felt she didn't have anybody with whom she could talk about her worries. Her parents did not understand her problem, Paula felt, because they did not care about social position. Mother would be the person to turn to, but Paula felt she did not understand. "Maybe she is the one who is off. Instead of saying that my aunt is wrong by being so snobbish, maybe we are the ones who are off." That was the first open criticism of her parents' attitude.

I reformulated what she had said, that it seemed that her father's family had snubbed her mother, who had reacted by saying "I don't care" instead of asserting herself: "I have a feeling that you tried to correct it but you didn't know how. I think it is too big a job for a little girl to set the social life of her whole family right." Paula then went into much detail about the pain of growing up in a small town where she felt not recognized as belonging to a leading family.

I explained to her the difficulties other anorexic girls run into. "Kids who have been very, very good the way you were—you were the pretty one, you were the smart one, you were the conscientious one, you were the helpful one, you really were top girl at home—and then they feel suddenly not truly recognized. Then they start this dieting business, losing weight, and suddenly the parents and everybody else focuses on them. Some like the attention they get that way—others do not."

She did not like this attention. "It makes me mad. I was mad about coming here, but now I am glad that I came." I added, "Because we have looked at things together. Sometimes kids don't want to give up the power they have in being so skinny." This she denied: "I don't really have any power, because I don't really feel like doing anything." I commented, "You have a lot of power." She objected, "Not really." I elaborated on this: "Exactly. It is not real power, but it looks like it. They are worried, but they can't tell you 'Eat, eat,' because then you throw a scene or have a temper tantrum, and that's power. You keep them quiet. They wanted to go on a vacation, and you said 'I don't want to go.' So they all stayed at home. That's power. But it isn't helpful power. What you need help with is to find your place where you belong, so that you have friends and can be a girl who enjoys life, a girl who feels good about herself— that's what you need help with. And being so skinny just interferes."

Paula replied rather desperately, "Why do I feel so fat?" (Her weight was below seventy pounds at that time.) I explained, "You think 'fat' means the same as 'not being good enough.' And that's what you fear, that you are not as good as you think you should be. Your great fear is that the 'right' people don't want you, that they don't respect you, that you don't have a social place. Maybe you have tried too hard to correct things. You call 'fat' everything you are dissatisfied with." She responded with a certain amount of relief and said spontaneously, "I want to eat just about everything and to start eating normally again." I encouraged her and repeated, "The things you need help with have nothing to do with food and dieting, or fat and weight. You have been the special girl in the family, and you feel responsible for your family. You really want to make Father and Mother happier, but you are scared that this is too big a job for you."

The next day the great news was that Paula had enjoyed her supper and eaten food for breakfast that she had not eaten for a long time. The main points of the previous session were openly discussed in a joint session with the parents. Paula's way of participating seemed to have changed. Instead of being shy and reluctant to express an opinion, she was quite outspoken in describing the whole family's dilemma. I encouraged her to be more open about these questions and more self-assertive about the situation. I informed the physician of my observations during the consultation and suggested that psychiatric help be sought from a medical school that was not too far away.

Jenny: Manipulator Par Excellence

In Jenny's case the consultation led me to conclude that the family's interaction was so disturbing that family therapy was indicated, in spite of the patient's age and the fact that she lived away from home.

Request for the consultation on this twenty-one-year-old woman came from her therapist. After nearly three years of therapy Jenny had made considerable progress in psychological understanding, but her weight had been slowly decreasing. I requested a more extensive report from the therapist and letters from the patient and her parents in which they could explain how they saw the development of the illness. The reports from the doctor and from Jenny came within a week or two, but I heard nothing from the parents. After repeated inquiry the mother wrote that they had never heard about this request but were eager to cooperate, and she wrote a very lengthy, meticulously detailed report on her daughter's development.

Jenny also had a sister two years older who had been plump as a child and had been harassed about it. Jenny had watched this and became excessively concerned when she gained some weight with menarche (at age eleven). At around fourteen or fifteen years she began to vomit regularly to control her weight. Then she cut down her food intake and her weight loss became a matter of concern. During her older sister's engagement, she had lost a great deal of weight. Despite her eating difficulties, she kept up her studies and was considering going into a Ph.D. program. While in psychotherapy she had moved away from her home and proved herself quite competent, except for the progressive weight loss. When her weight dropped below 70 pounds she was hospitalized on a psychiatric service, where she managed to lose eight more pounds, to a low of 61 pounds. It was at this time that consultation was requested.

When Jenny and her parents came to Houston several weeks later her weight was 63 pounds and she looked severely malnourished and physically wasted. Medical hospitalization seemed urgently indicated. I explained that no valid psychological exploration could take place as long as she was in a state of serious starvation. Jenny pleaded to postpone hospitalization for a few days so that she could be alone with her parents, for the first time in her life, and could enjoy the luxury of hotel living. This was agreed to, and during this time she went on a real eating spree. Without difficulty she ate meat, seafood, delicatessen food, mainly in gourmet restaurants. She gained several pounds during this week while staying with her parents at the hotel but then stopped eating after she was admitted to the hospital. She would talk in glowing terms about how much she enjoyed food, how much she ate, but her weight did not increase.

Several family sessions clarified the extent of family tension, which had been only hinted at by the confusion about the parents' letter. In the family sessions, there was not only continuous interrupting and contradiction of anything anyone said but also disagreement about basic facts. I give one example: the mother said that she felt concern not only about Jenny's weight loss but also about her unhappiness. Jenny interrupted her, stating that currently she did not feel unhappy at all but in fact felt very happy and very active. The father then made a disclaimer that her happiness was not the point at issue. Strained interaction became apparent with every topic, be it a matter of health, education, behavior of the other children, or the family's social standing. After one week the parents returned to their hometown and Jenny stayed on at the medical service.

Anorexic patients are considered manipulative and devious, but in a way Jenny deserves the prize. She gave such conflicting and contradictory information in messages she took back and forth to the medical service that I found it necessary to phone the internist after each conference to tell him what had been discussed. She gave her parents glowing reports about how much she was improving, though during the first few weeks she did not gain any weight at all but was engaged in competitive struggles with other anorexic patients and with the nurses. When confronted with her manipulative behavior, she acknowledged it. She began to eat again and her weight rose during the next few weeks, reaching 80 pounds five weeks after her arrival in Houston. Everybody appeared to be delighted with what was going on, mostly Jenny herself, and she decided on her own that she would stay in Houston, continue her studies here, and be in ambulatory therapy with me. She wrote her parents that this was the treatment plan, convinced the internist that this had been agreed on—only I did not know about it.

During her medical hospitalization, I saw her regularly in sessions that were used to reevaluate her whole development, including the use she had made of her illness. This evaluation revealed that in her home there had been much tension and disharmony throughout her life. She was aware of the tension between her parents and had taken sides with both, at various times, but had withdrawn during the last few years. I concluded that Jenny had little chance of developing into a self-reliant person as long as the family struggles went unresolved. I therefore urgently recommended treatment for the family. If this proved unacceptable (or unavailable in their home community), Jenny would need residential treatment where she could work out her inner insecurity and anxiety without arousing continuous concern and conflict in others. Even though I had expressed this clearly to the parents, in telephone calls as well as in letters, the pressure persisted to make me accept Jenny as an ambulatory patient while she was living in Houston, a strange city where she had no contacts. Finally we located an experienced family therapist in a larger city near her hometown. Jenny and her parents consented to seek help there.

This plan worked well. After several years Jenny seemed to have developed true self-reliance and independence. She maintained the weight gain she had made while in Houston and gradually achieved a normal weight.

CHAPTER 4

Getting Involved

———

PATIENTS with anorexia nervosa have the reputation of offering unusual treatment problems, ranging from rejecting treatment altogether to provoking dangerous life-threatening situations by refusing food or displaying other behaviors incompatible with physical health. These patients are often in the psychotherapist's office under duress, and they may feel that they have been taken from one doctor to another to be fixed like a malfunctioning appliance. In this chapter I will attempt to show how I understand the anorexic's behavior and attitudes and how I try to engage the anorexic in psychotherapy or consultation.

In many cases the patient's behavior in treatment is a re-enactment of the relationship to the parents. This relationship may involve keeping the parents from interfering with the patient's starvation program while at the same time preventing them from feeling that they deserve blame or criticism for their treatment of the patient. Feeling that the parents want to be kind and considerate, the daughter is under continuous strain to outguess them and to show that she has viewed their actions as "kind and considerate." This results in the patient's rigidly good behavior and double-track thinking, reflecting the moral judgment of a very young child. This type of thinking (pursuing one's own thoughts while trying simultaneously to figure out parental motives and reactions) is characteristic of anorexics, even of those with occasional episodes of disobedience or angry disagreement.

This attitude is carried over to treatment, and the seemingly cooperative, conforming behavior that many patients display—even though they may have openly stated that they do not need or want treatment—slows down the therapeutic exploration. The act of "undoing" that is so common in treatment with anorexics is related to this attitude. In "undoing," the patients will agree to some point, even elaborate on something that has been clarified, speak about it as if it reflects their own thinking (only to revert from it later), and, within a few days or weeks, act and talk as if nothing has ever been learned. Many are so subtle in this seeming agreement and undoing that it is difficult for the therapist to help the patient to clarify what she is doing.

As mentioned, practically all anorexics I see have been in treatment with someone else and have been referred because progress was slow or had come to a standstill. This raises the questions of what is so difficult about these patients and why do things miscarry with them so often. There are, of course, many different reasons for failures or arrests in psychotherapy, and various aspects need to be clarified in each individual case. However, I have been impressed by how frequently it looks as if the therapists have been intimidated by these patients. This intimidation may be the result of their potentially life-threatening physical situation or their stalwart refusal to admit to a problem or to the capacity to change. I relate the fact that I have been able to establish rapport with at least some anorexic patients to the fact that by being aware of the possibility of being intimidated, I acknowledge its presence and its power. I communicate this possibility to the patient and family, thus conveying that while I refuse to be intimidated, I want to look at why and how they use this method of relating to the people who want to be helpful to them.

Why do these patients use this intimidating style of interaction? Deeply convinced of their own ineffectiveness, these youngsters can experience a sense of power, of being in control, of getting attention and consideration, only by arousing fear and apprehension in those responsible for their care. At the same time these actions cause them to become more and more imprisoned in an invalid way of life. The therapeutic task is to cut through this pseudopower and to help them develop their own inner capacities for true independence, so that they no longer need to exercise power through weakness or through the tyranny of fear. I let it be known that I am relatively little impressed by or sympathetic to a patient's dramatic display of helplessness. As soon as possible I try to recognize and focus on her potential for independent self-expression. The important point is to convey to an anorexic that she is not helpless, though many abilities or potentials have remained undeveloped. A crucial issue in treatment is to permit patients to feel more competent, more capable to develop their capacities, and less the result of what other people have done to them.

The therapist's task is to be objective yet personal and warm. It is important that the inquiry is not carried out in an accusing way or with the intent of pointing out hostility or aggression. In an indirect way the therapist must convey to the patient that her problems are human and understandable, and what matters are the human qualities. Yet there is also the need to communicate to a patient that severe malnutrition interferes with her psychic functioning and therefore diminishes the usefulness of psychotherapy.

The therapist must be aware that the patient, though seemingly speaking in rational language, may use words and concepts with a different perspective of reality. Others may or may not interpret this communication style as a sign of deceitfulness; I do not consider it so. For reasons central to their developmental problems, these patients have gotten along with—or gotten *away* with—unclear use of language or deviating meaning for a long time. They take correction or alternative suggestions with regard to their language as criticism. Therefore, clarifying and translating into realistic language what the patient expresses in her often distorted language is a very slow process, but it is necessary to help her recognize and, even more, reevaluate her customary, outdated way of speaking and thinking.

While the onset of the anorexic illness involves what looks like drastic changes in behavior and thinking, it is of utmost importance to reconstruct with a patient what had been going on *before* the hunger illness, with its far-reaching effects, overshadowed the psychological picture. This involves evaluating childhood experience and the significant people not only in terms of factual events but in the way a growing child experienced them. What needs to be clarified is not so much the content of the experience as the style and relatedness in which they were expressed. Although this of course is done in intensive psychotherapy with other patients, the contrast between the current behavior and earlier attitudes is unusually strong in anorexia nervosa, and it is complicated by the psychological effects of the starvation.

Even when the interviews proceed in a way to support the patient's competence, to circumvent the problems with intimidation, and to clarify the patient's developmental misperception without suggesting deceit, difficulties often arise. Many patients cannot tolerate the idea that there are things they do not know but need to learn, cannot admit evidence of something wrong with their thinking and reasoning, and become anxious and angry by the very fact that something new has come up. During the initial interviews I frequently can tell whether the needed degree of openness and patience will develop between the patient and me to allow restrained, inhibited communication to develop into a free and trusting therapeutic interchange.

The following vignettes illustrate the development of therapeutic communication with three anorexic patients.

Annette: Dealing with Guilt

After the initial extended consultation and hospitalization for weight gain, Annette returned to college with plans to begin intensive psychotherapy after she received her undergraduate degree. Over the three years of her treatment I saw her three (and then later two) times a week for treatment.

In the consultation, I had explained that it was urgent that Annette maintain her weight. She had been pleased with the higher weight she achieved. She maintained her weight fairly well during college, but when she returned to begin therapy it had dropped below 80 pounds. I did not compromise on the agreed-on condition that meaningful therapy could be carried out only if her weight was in a more adequate range. She agreed to hospitalization for intravenous hyperalimentation, actively participated in the program, and supplemented it by eating solid food. Her weight rose to nearly 100 pounds within two weeks, and she maintained it at 95 pounds for several months. During this time she became involved in intensive psychotherapy.

Annette's explanation for her recent weight loss was typically anorexic. She had spent several weeks visiting old friends and relatives, and she felt obliged to maintain her "image," namely, that of a person who ate very little. She explained that she could not possibly eat more than a particular person had seen her eat before. "Maintaining her image in the eyes of others" played an enormous role in Annette's life and was a serious problem in treatment. This stance actually prohibited or denied changes that were taking place in spite of herself. It reflected her deep conviction of not having a personality or identity of her own, of experiencing herself only as a reflection of other people's views of her, while she remained "empty," a "nothing."

In her sessions Annette was exceedingly polite, proper, obedient, and restrained in any emotional expressions. She showed little spontaneity but answered questions appropriately. She was much too polite and well bred not to answer questions or to describe what was going on. Her overt behavior said nothing about her inner experience or inner opposition to treatment. She expressed few emotions in general and was restrained in her reaction to me, most reluctant to disagree with me or to express anger or disappointment. A few times she left the office without saying goodbye, or by slamming the door; she never verbalized anger openly. She lived with the attitude "I cannot help feeling anger, but I certainly can help showing it." She cried only rarely when painful memories or conclusions came up.

Though she was more relaxed than during the acute starvation period of the year prior to treatment, she sat stiffly upright on the couch or in a chair for more than a year. It was quite an event when one day she let go and leaned back, saying, "It feels good to sit down and relax." She was surprised when I acknowledged this ability to relax as something new. During her treatment I would acknowledge any signs of new behavior or greater spontaneity endless times.

In my role as therapist I try to be explicit in what I expect a comment to convey, or I outline what I consider expectable experiences, something anybody must have undergone as a physical fact or an emotional reaction. Annette never openly disagreed with any such truisms or generalizations, but many years later she confessed that she had never believed a word when I made some optimistic statement about childhood. I indicated, for instance, that a child has the right to expect to be well treated, encouraged, and confirmed according to her developmental needs by the grown-ups in her life. When this type of remark came up she would listen to it as something a doctor would say to make her feel better, but she did not believe that this was a meaningful concept of how a child needs to be treated.

Annette had grown up in a well-functioning home, where she had received excellent care. She agreed on the whole with the picture her parents had described, that of a peaceful, polite, and devoted family, in which nobody ever raised his or her voice or showed anger or dissatisfaction. She herself remembered that once she had heard a comment that made a deep impression on her. It concerned another girl who was described as always cheerful, with a smile on her face. To Annette that was the highest praise, and she aspired to deserve the same comment. So the parents' description of her as a smiling, cheerful child was correct, and Annette agreed, but later she added that this picture left out the underlying pain and distress it created. The overall impression one gained from talking about her relations with various family members was that of enormous restraint and great inhibition to communicate.

Annette was convinced that the grown-ups never meant what they said, that they did their duty by her and would hide their resentment at having to take care of her. She felt that it was one of her tasks in life to be modest, not to be in the way or make demands. This was rarely stated openly but could be deduced from material she brought up.

In many different situations I used the childhood anecdote about Annette not calling when she was through napping as an illustration of her inability to be spontaneous and self-assertive. While avoiding open or implied criticism she attributed this inability to her relationship to her parents, individually and as a couple. She always felt that she knew what her parents were really thinking (and that was that they were obeying the rules for proper behavior learned in their own youth) even though they might act or speak differently, in a more liberal and permissive vein. She remained convinced that they would have resented it if she had asked questions or needed their help in other ways; therefore she avoided doing so.

Double-track thinking became clear in her attitude toward her various college roommates. She would never say anything outright that might bother the other person, but often she was silently angry and could not understand that the other person felt differently. She felt that any evidence of neglect, or of someone's not doing her part, reflected the other person's very unfriendly feelings toward her.

She was certain that other people never truly said what they felt, and she made great efforts not to show anger openly. One day leaving work, she pinned a slip to a cabinet requesting greater tidiness from her coworkers. When I remarked that one might assume that she carried within herself, though probably outside of her awareness, an enormous reservoir of anger, resentment, and even feelings of vengefulness, she answered sharply that she had never had such feelings and added with conviction, "I hope not, and I hope I never will."

Despite this protest she began to gain some appreciation for the negative role played by this inhibition of feelings in her life. I asked repeatedly why she constantly used such expressions as "I had to . . . ," as if she felt obligated. She never made a personal protest. She explained, "When I do have anger I would never express it, which is one of the roots of the whole thing. So whenever I was angry and I felt like saying 'Go mind your own business,' I wouldn't do it, but I would act it anyway. But I never, never, never would have attacked anyone the way Eve does." (Eve was another anorexic on the service.) She added, "Maybe some of the agitation I have felt about going home is that I can in a way imagine that I am turning thirteen, that I am going to be the obnoxious teenager that parents tear their hair about because now she has become an adolescent with all those horrors—saying 'No' and 'I won't' and 'What I want to do—.' I know they're going to be mightily surprised when I arrive home and walk in the door. I am just tired of being compliant." I commented that it sounded as if she had developed more self-reliance and become more self-assertive. To this she agreed, stating that her combative feelings might protect her from letting the good feelings crumble. "It has been a battle to get this far. I'm not about to let it go away. I won't let it slip back into the old routine, and that means I am really going to fight against it."

As therapy progressed Annette recognized that it was very

difficult for her to differentiate between what she had "thought" about her parents and other significant people during her developing years and what she had just assumed was their attitude: "I have never expressed my wants, never took advantage of anything, never said that I wanted to do this or that." She was very reluctant to examine the factors that had made her so intimidated, so unsure of her own worth and rights. She added, "I always felt guilty when anyone did anything for me that I could have done myself. If I go beyond a certain point I feel like I'm treading on thin ice. I really do not know what the other person expects." But in spite of her reluctance there was gradual progress, and she began to face issues more directly and to integrate them into a more realistic way of life.

Her low self-esteem was a great issue during treatment. She spoke of herself as "the scum of the earth" and was rather unyielding about talking about herself in more positive terms. She gradually gave up tearing herself down so severely, even admitting at times (albeit without much conviction at first) that she might have some positive qualities. She could accept (so it seemed to me at the time) that eventually she might be able to lead a self-respecting, fulfilling life. However, one day when she was rather depressed she confessed that she still had a feeling that there was something "embarrassing and black" in her. This "blackness" became a recurrent theme, but one that I felt more comfortable exploring when Annette was in a more positive state of mind.

One day she talked about an unusually enjoyable weekend, when she had felt in good rapport with other people. But even this pleasant report had ended up with her comparing herself, unfavorably, to Josie, the sister in whose presence she had always felt uncomfortable, even now as an adult. I explained to her that children, after having been hurt repeatedly, tend to approach a new situation with the same person with a certain expectation of rebuff. That seemed to be going on in her relationship with Josie. Whenever she had any dealings with her she expected to get hurt and had to restrain the hostile feelings that this aroused in her. Instead of defending Josie as she had in the past, saying that she had never done anything wrong to her and that it was unjust to blame her, Annette went along with the inquiry and this time she enlarged on several points, how angry, hurt, and ridiculed she had felt.

I intended to continue this theme in the next session. In the past Annette had repeatedly disclaimed such open inquiry, and each time we had start all over again. During the next session, however, she opened with this theme. She looked more animated than usual when she entered the office and then began immediately: "It's amazing, what you said yesterday about my not really knowing Josie, always approaching her expecting to be hurt, has now made me very curious. It is almost as if I want to go and meet her, you know, like a new person, 'Who are you?'—Well, it's almost like meeting a stranger, I mean the way I feel, as if I had been told about this person and now I'm curious to meet her and see what she is like in the flesh rather than what somebody else has told me." I reminded her that the "somebody who told her" was her own disturbed and distorted memory. To this she agreed: "I guess I'm saying I want to meet her as a stranger because in the past I was dealing with a person I was looking for." Annette elaborated how she had always related to this sister in terms of superiority and inferiority and how she had always compared herself to her, always coming out second best.

I explained to her at this point how children may sometimes find themselves confronted by insoluble dilemmas, in which there is danger of getting hurt no matter what they do. If they let it be known how upset and pained they feel, they might be faced with the greater danger of losing the love and care of the people on whom they are most dependent. "Yesterday you said not once but twice that one cannot squash a sister. When you experienced her rejection you must have felt extremely angry at her, but you lived by the rule that one must love one's sister. Therefore you were unable to protest or make your own demands." Annette added, "At the same time I was working so hard to get any approval from her, anything she could give me." Annette agreed that avoiding her sister's hatred had been a dominant theme in her life. She elaborated on the difficulty of reconstructing and knowing whether her feelings were correct: "I would like to talk about what you said before. I almost don't know what to think about my own perceptions of Josie, knowing now that they were incorrect. I mean, I almost don't feel the need for having to blame her for being a mean sister. I don't even know if she was a mean sister."

She went on, "Now today—it may change tomorrow—I sort of have the feeling, 'Well, I don't really care what she was and what I felt.' That's what I call settling myself in regard to members of the family. I have done it with the others, in particular with Father and the older ones. When I say 'I want to meet her as a stranger,' I feel I want her to know that I am new too. If she doesn't like me, well, that's too bad, that's not my problem anymore. It's her problem."

I felt it was important to learn how this experience affected her self-concept. "Does it help you to handle your self-punishing attitude better? Are you kinder to yourself if you understand why you were justified in having angry feelings?" This time she agreed: "Yes, I no longer have to feel guilty about having felt hurt. I no longer have to feel that I have to worry about her, always putting myself down, wanting to get even. I mean, she is no longer representing something that makes me feel antagonistic every time I look at it or think about it. The antagonism has gone out of it." I added, "And it was the antagonism that you felt you had to hide. Can you imagine how it will be if Josie and you meet as new people?" She replied, "I feel almost the same now with Josie as if I hadn't known her before. She is related by blood, but I had been basing my whole knowing about her on just a tiny fraction of what she is." Earlier she had described how she had felt that every friendliness that was shown to her by a family member was really a fraud, that Josie was the only one who had expressed how negatively they all felt about her. "It's almost as if this whole weight had been taken away from me. It was what I was doing to myself in relation to thinking about her. It is no longer of importance, because she is not in charge of my life and I don't have to judge myself thinking she is judging me, which is all very complicated. I would think of anything I had done and would say automatically, 'It's not so great; look what she can do.' It was often like that—in comparison I could always make Josie look better." I repeated what she had said: "If you really feel this way now, then we can say that we made a great step forward yesterday. You recognize how such a misdirection of one's view of someone else comes about." And she elaborated, "And you look at the other person only to find her always in a hurtful context. I mean, I really couldn't see Josie, I mean emotionally. I see now the whole thing is so childish, the way I have carried anything I may have experienced through all this time. Maybe when I was little I didn't think about what I was seeing—I carried it on through life and made it the only thing I ever saw. Yesterday, at three o'clock, it changed. Incredible, just wild. The most liberating thing I can see and say is 'I don't care about her, I don't care about what she thinks of me and I don't care what I think she thinks.' What had been ruining me was my not being able to step out of my age level, ten, twelve, what have you, carrying all that stuff around with me, all the way back and not permitting anything else to be different."

This statement is probably as clearly as anyone can describe the intermixing of realistic observation and unrealistic interpretation of one's own thinking. When Annette said "my not being able to step out of my age level," it had meaning to her. I had not confronted her with the fact that her thinking was immature. It was genuinely her experience that these feelings and reactions were not in line with her adult thinking.

During this whole discussion Annette had been unusually lively and assertive. She had used the word "liberating" and she acted much freer. She even opened up a new theme, eager and willing to enlarge on something she had mentioned in an offhand way. "A few weeks ago I was talking about how I felt about the rest of the world, as if I were on the island." Now she went into detail: "Josie was standing on the bridge and would not permit me to get off my island. I always had the feeling it was her or me. If I wanted to get over I would have to chuck her over the bridge and she would drown. But for her to be acceptable to the rest of the world she had to make sure that I stayed on the island."

I remarked that one could understand now why she had hesitated to talk about such vindictive images, adding, "No child is born to be a murderer or to hurt her sister." She confirmed, "I know—that's why I was so reluctant to approach her or to talk about her. But the only way I thought I could save myself was to get rid of her." We went into detail about how many of her feelings about Josie were realistic and came from her own guilt over having such negative feelings. "There was something the matter with me, and that made me feel so angry toward her." This I confirmed, "As if your feelings toward her were proof of your own wrongness"; and she elaborated, "I mean, a civilized human being who was basically brought up to be a nice person, how can she really express her feelings?"

I related Annette's deep sense of her inner blackness to her guilt over these previously hidden anger feelings. Now that her secret feelings were in the open, one might expect that she would look at herself and the world differently. I asked, "Doesn't it feel like a better world?" And she eagerly replied, "Gosh, yes." She continued with the image of the bridge: "No matter how much antagonism I feel, I could not commit 'sistercide' or whatever it is."

She continued: "The other thing I wanted to say about the word 'black' and the associations I have to it was the feeling of being different, this knowing the attitude of myself toward myself. The worst is that I really feel I am not myself, and this is really sick, this not being myself, not my body or person, not really a human being. And that is what is really weird."

Ida: A Crack in the Wall

Like most anorexics, Ida expressed genuine resistance to the idea of therapy. The therapist's task is to accept this resistance respectfully and to be supportive of it, but he or she must also explain that the pursuit of psychotherapy offers the patient something to gain personally. Ida's good behavior helped insofar as she would not refuse to talk, but it stood in the way because she accepted everything politely without expressing her true feelings. Ida felt strongly that too many people worried about her weight; this made it harder to eat. She complained, "They say, 'You look so thin, blah, blah, blah, and we feel so worried about you.' I would never have thought of treatment for myself. I always admired slim people, then I wanted to be slim myself, I went on a diet, and I feel very normal now. I consider other people's concern just a difference in taste. At first I didn't even recognize that I was not in good health." In answer to my question she defined "high weight" as "anything above what I am right now."

I like to use early sessions to familiarize myself with the reality of the patient's living conditions. For Ida, this now meant residing in the college dormitory and having a sense of strangeness in living away from home. She had traveled a great deal and had a more international background than most students. I also examined the style of her social interactions, the extent of her activities, and in particular her attitude toward nutrition. While becoming familiar with various aspects of her background I pursued as the main question "How did you get this way?" It meant becoming acquainted with the outer facts of her early upbringing and family life, but even more, recognizing the experiences that had been distressing or handicapping in her early development.

Ida showed more than average interest in reviewing her early development and in the reconstruction of her background. She expressed pride in the superiority of her home and family. She was the younger of two children, her brother being six years older. There was also a much older half sister from her father's first marriage. Her father had been a top executive in an international corporation and also had rendered important public service. Ida knew from family discussions that her father had adored his first daughter but then she had become a disappointment to him. Throughout her life Ida felt that *she* must not let her father down. She was sure it had been a keen disappointment for him that she was born a girl. She felt that not so much was expected of her as of her brother, and it became a matter of great importance to her to prove herself as outstanding as she felt he was. In another context she told me about her father's worrying about her becoming too flirtatious when she was a young teenager. She had decided that she would be the opposite of her half sister, and she changed her behavior accordingly.

The greatest tragedy of Ida's life had been her father's sudden death at age sixty-six when she was twelve years old. Ida brought up memories in relation to this. She was aware of the change his death had implied in her life. "Shortly before my father died, we stopped having governesses, and then I started seeing more of my mother. I began to understand a little bit more about the world, and I started hearing about business things and why my mother was constantly worried."

In Ida's recollections about her father's death she also expressed much pride in her family and went into many details, at times in a somewhat condescending tone, to reassure me that there was nothing wrong with her, and that in spite of certain small disagreements her home had been perfect. Her speaking of hating herself was the first admission that she suffered from true inner distress and severe basic dissatisfaction. I formulated this in several ways to her, each time with a reassuring statement that as we got to know each other she would find out where she felt she had been disregarded or neglected in some way. The goal of therapy for her would be to encourage her undeveloped qualities, all the potential that she had never developed. The central theme of the subsequent inquiry was to discover why she suffered from such severe self-hatred for having regained a small amount of the previously lost weight.

As noted before, Ida was hospitalized medically early in her treatment. She was discharged from the hospital when her weight had reached 80 pounds, with the agreement that she would be readmitted if she could not maintain her weight above that figure. For the next few months her weight remained marginal. She was seen regularly by her internist, who reported that when there had been a gain in weight she would mutter, "I hate it, I hate it," and that she felt "heavy all over" and "guilty like a robber for breaking the law." It looked as if she needed more personal attention, and I seriously considered whether she needed the services of a long-term residential treatment center. Her current living conditions appeared precarious. The college was not prepared to supervise her poor eating, sleeplessness, and overactivity. She herself was deaf to any suggestion to cut down on her course load or to be less active. I explained to her that my concern for her physical safety might interfere with the psychotherapeutic process. It is of interest that when we reviewed her progress in treatment much later, she mentioned that the strongest factor that kept her from discontinuing treatment or losing more weight was the possibility of losing the opportunity to talk about herself in therapy. These talks were very important to her, right from the beginning. It was the first time that somebody had truly listened to what she had to say, and she soon recognized that talking about her feelings helped her to feel better.

Ida came to her treatment sessions regularly. Though she used much time for complaining about being forced to maintain such a high weight, she began to talk somewhat more freely about her background, expressing great admiration for the superiority of everybody in her family and much self-accusation for being unworthy in comparison, for she could never hope to live up to their expectations. Her parents had been very active socially, and she spent time with them only during weekends or vacations. She was praised for her skill and courage at sports, keeping up with her older brother and his group of friends.

In mid-October, about six weeks after therapy had begun, Ida's brother visited and took part in a general discussion of her treatment needs. She had barely maintained her weight at 80 pounds, and the question of long-term hospitalization was being discussed. She objected to this plan but stated at the same time that she doubted whether she could do it on her own. "It's not easy to go up in weight, and it's not easy to stop laxatives. That's why I am here. If I were a normal person I wouldn't be here."

She repeatedly expressed the implied reproach, "You are not doing enough for me." She expected that therapy would change her, but at the same time she complained that she was being controlled and that people made decisions for her: "You won't let me do anything. You don't treat me like an independent adult person; you coerce me." Interestingly, in the presence of her brother she was much more outspoken and angry than she had ever shown when I saw her alone.

Ida subsequently went home for the Thanksgiving weekend and came back "practically recovered," in her words. She had "fallen in love" with one of her brother's friends. She also had enjoyed eating during the holidays, and her weight had risen to 83 pounds. From then on her weight stayed safely above 80 pounds. The "flight into health" through "being in love," however, did not last. When she went home for Christmas vacation, she recognized that she was severely depressed, unable to feel comfortable with other young people or even in her mother's home. She wrote a letter trying to describe her depression: "With my gaining weight I am starting to get bad depressions at night, so bad that I cry into my pillow. These depressions are rather recent. . . . Today I felt again this peculiar sensation, that I know everybody loves me but I can't understand why." She then described a half dream in which she and several of her friends were walking on a beautiful mountain road when she suddenly jumped, without reason, into the empty space and then saw herself smashed on the rocks—but felt no pain. She was puzzled by the expression of horror on her friends' faces. "It was then that I woke up from my semisleep and I started really crying and hating myself, immediately feeling my stomach was *full* and *fat.* I just lay there hating myself."

Writing and sending this letter represented a definite step forward in her commitment to therapy: it was the first time that she openly shared with me the depth of her despair and her fear of her own destructive impulses. She had had much resistance against exploring the handicapping and constructive aspects of her early life. This letter was like a crack in a seemingly insurmountable wall.

Ida had grown up with definite inhibitions against expressing emotions. No one in her home ever raised his or her voice, except her older brother, who would fight with the governesses. She herself had never raised her voice or expressed anger openly. Though she was encouraged to do so in therapy, she was much too polite to express negative feelings or disagreement. The only exception had been her emotions in the joint session with her brother. In the beginning of our work I mentioned jokingly what I would consider signs of progress: that she would flunk a course and would shout at me so loudly that the secretary could hear it. Neither of these events happened, though finally she did drop a course because the topic did not interest her and she felt it was a burden.

The fact that she avoided arguments proved to be a great handicap in therapy. Whatever point came up (except when food was involved), she would go along or at least would not openly object. However, her general attitude expressed a sense of superiority, an unspoken "I know better," setting the stage for the process of undoing. She also hated to cry in front of people. She had never truly let go and cried at the time of her father's death. There were always people around and she didn't even feel safe in her room, because someone might come in unexpectedly. She had insisted on having a single room at college, fearing that she might reveal her feelings in the presence of a roommate. It was a long time before she permitted herself to cry in the therapy sessions when sad and disturbing memories came up.

Her work and attendance in college progressed smoothly. She seemed to enjoy her courses and conscientiously kept up with her studies, making sure that she was acknowledged and recognized as someone who contributed to the discussions. She had chosen courses in which she was truly interested; this stood in contrast to her earlier school career, when she had been highly competitive with her brother, who had attended a private high school that stressed mathematics and science. She had insisted on going to this same school though she had little talent or interest in these subjects, but she tried to force herself to keep up with him. Finally she transferred to a high school that emphasized arts and the humanities. She did very well there but did not take pride in it because "if it is easy, then there is no merit in it." However, in college she decided on courses that meshed with her special talents and interests.

Socially she kept to herself, though she would talk of "friends." I recognized how severely she had isolated herself only later, when Ida and I reviewed her whole history. This was a continuation of a pattern she had created at home; she did not take part in any social activities but would spend most of her time in her own room, studying. If other girls came to her room or were otherwise too social, she would withdraw to the library to be completely undisturbed. She also studied long hours. Much later she would explain that when she was at a low weight her capacity to concentrate and memorize was greatly impaired and studying took much longer than when she was better nourished.

Lucy: "I Never Cared Much About Honesty"

The question of honesty plays a larger role in anorexia nervosa than in most mental conditions. In Lucy's case honesty became the key issue. It is important to differentiate distortion from deceitfulness or dishonesty. The most basic distortion is the anorexic patient's inability to see the world realistically. Therefore, her explanations or statements, while not according to the facts, are not deliberate lies, but are instead part of the illness or developmental delay. These distortions in thinking require endless examination in order for the therapist to help the patient see herself and the world more realistically. Active forms of deceit, such as the patient's intentional misrepresentation of activities or denial of events, may be a lesser part of the therapeutic picture. Lucy displayed both problems.

Lucy was twenty years old when she came for consultation. She had become anorexic three years earlier while at a boarding school where she felt out of place. She had been in treatment (including inpatient treatment) previously, but things had not progressed well. When questioned, she described how in the last treatment setting she had not gone beyond the point of talking only about those topics that she felt her doctor wanted to hear. I expressed the hope that she might be more genuine with me.

In Lucy's therapy there were many examples of active deceit—for example, talking about a job she had never had or classes she had cut. She was usually open about the deceit afterward, explaining that being truthful in the first place would have caused too much upheaval. We had an open discussion about genuineness when an example of gross dishonesty was discovered.

Lucy was a college student, and she planned her three-week vacation to coincide with the time I took off for my own vacation. She informed me of a change of plans, that her parents wanted to take the whole family on trip. She came back four weeks later, full of enthusiasm about all the marvelous things she had seen, but stated that the trip had been cut short. By chance I received a letter from someone in her hometown that mentioned that Lucy's family trip had been canceled altogether. She confirmed this when asked, explaining that her parents had had to stay home. She described the process of her deception: "I really did believe it. I convinced myself that we had gone. I started thinking about Paris and convinced myself that we had gone." She then commented that her father had been against this deception, while her mother had supported it. She spoke about the contradiction in her mother, who on the one hand considered therapy terribly important and encouraged Lucy but who also did not hesitate to support her in staying away from therapy during the cancelled vacation. Lucy felt that this deceitfulness had been carried on from mother to daughter through several generations in her family. She went into great detail about how her mother's social attitude had been, to her, an instruction in dishonesty. Lucy felt that the deception that goes on during the development of the anorexic illness is all-pervasive but usually more subtle.

Lucy had begun to eat freely shortly after coming into treatment, and we had discussed repeatedly what she had felt during the starvation period. She had complained constantly about "feeling full," of not being able to eat more. She stated without hesitation: "It is a big lie—nobody can prove that you don't feel full." I felt this was too simplistic an explanation, that much more than a simple lie was involved. She went on to explain, "You are living like in a trance. For yourself you have tunnel vision. That's all there is to it. You lose sight of what you are really like, though with other people you can see exactly what is going on. It is just like this: you are safe in your narrow tunnel, but nowhere else—you can't believe how absurd the thinking is. I was continuously preoccupied with what I looked like to others, like when I went into an elevator." She explained: "There were too many strong demands and I had too weak a self-image. Really I had no self-image. I literally knew nothing about myself and how I had developed. My relationship to my parents comes into it. The motto was always 'Spare Mother,' and I wouldn't bother her with things that troubled me."

As mentioned earlier, Lucy had been at boarding school when the anorexia began, and she explained: "I couldn't find a way out—it was the wrong place for me, but once I started to lose weight, I totally forgot about everything else. You are depriving yourself—you are starving to death—and you tell yourself it is beautiful. Everybody presses you to eat more, and that is when your tunnel vision comes in. I have a feeling sex would break it down, but when you are starving you don't feel anything. It is unbelievable what it does to your body. You are always preoccupied with food—but also how you look. It is so easy to say you are 'full'—it is a lie—it is only a justification. You have to deny yourself food. You can't say 'I want to be skinny,' not really, so you have to come up with a reason for everybody else. So you say you are full. It is easy to say, 'I can't eat that much.' "

Several months later she spoke about it again in a different context: "I have to make an excuse for everything I do. And I think when you really break down and lose the weight—no one can stand to live that way. I think that is where the self-deception comes in, because to keep yourself well—for me, anyway—I think it keeps me from being depressed, the self-deception and all the other deceptions." I commented that I had heard this before, this feeling of "When I am unhappy, then I lose weight and it makes me feel that I am worthwhile." She replied, "Yes, it's the same deceptive process. Saying I'm worthwhile because I lose weight requires lying to yourself, just like saying you are not hungry when you're starving."

She went on: "One reason why I lose weight is because I think, I really do think, I'm trying to punish myself. I have the feeling right now, that's why I think it's so important to talk about it—that it is a punishment. If I do that, then none of those other things will happen to me. You don't think of the ridiculousness of it either. It is just that it gives me that feeling—it is a very strange feeling, it is a physical feeling. It is almost like you know that you are hurting yourself, your body can feel it, and you deny that feeling." She felt starvation might protect her against having an accident or being involved in a tragedy. "Well, it seems like I'm using starvation as an excuse—it is hard to explain. I think that might be part of the feeling that you get of control and perfection, because you know what you're doing. You do know. I always knew what I was doing. Your body tells you all the time."

I inquired about her history of deceitfulness. "Let me tell you," she said, "I can't remember the day that I started doing it, but I started very young. I didn't think I was good enough. I thought I had to be better than I was. I had to make myself look better to other people. Looking better comes two different ways—you either have to really deceive yourself and make yourself look better, or you have to try harder in actual things. I wish now I would have *tried harder* more often. I think it would have been a lot healthier."

She gave more examples and I commented, "So there is in this self-deception really the denial of your own abilities in order to maintain the pretense that they are higher than they really are, while you are at the same time convinced they are less than your true gifts."

Lucy then returned to the idea of honesty: "I want to be really honest. Now, I have never thought about honesty in my whole life. I never thought it had any virtue at all; I never cared much about honesty. But I think if I worked more toward honesty, then I would think a little bit more about when I deceive myself. I think it starts with me deceiving myself, then deceiving other people. But sometimes, like with my parents, when we start talking about something I will tell an untruth and then I will start to believe it."

Lucy provided many examples of an anorexic's reliance on the ideas of others rather than her own feelings to explain her behaviors. She had seen the movie *The Exorcist* during her previous hospitalization for anorexia and subsequently described a certain parallel between creativity and the starvation high. She said that she had experienced something like visions, at least "strange things." While she was aware that these "strange things" occurred when she was in the hospital, "extremely starving," she thought she was "possessed by the devil" instead of attributing this to her bodily deprivation. She also described how she distorted her human feelings of fear into a political position. Describing her return home she said, "When we would go on outings, I was really afraid. I was like a little baby that is lost in a big crowd. Whenever we got around more than ten people I got very upset. I didn't think of people being in those cars, as human beings. They were these big things that made me feel afraid. I started to think about people in masses. I started thinking about ecology and how much all these people are ruining everything. We are ruining this earth. I became one of those hot-headed college students."

Lucy also spoke about her illness: "The last three years have been such a withdrawal for me. I can't understand what I'm afraid of. If it were physical danger, or if it were actual fear of being raped or getting killed, I could understand it. But the fear that I have is so irrational. I am never going to prove it to be a lie unless I go out and start talking to people. It doesn't really matter what I do—have lunch, talk about how horrible the dogs are—it doesn't make any difference. But that irrational fear is going to keep on growing until I go out there and prove I'm not lying again. I have this great unbelievable fear of people not liking me. That is as plain as I can put it." I pointed out to her that this had a counterpart—namely, the conviction that "I'm not worthy of their liking me"—and that this was just as much a lie. I explained, "That's what I call a basic misconception. You and this 'Anorexia Incorporated' have exactly the same fear: 'The way I am, I am not good enough, people won't like me.'" Lucy replied, "How can that ever be proven false unless you go out there and talk to people? That's what I'm beginning to realize, but I have to prove it. It is almost on the same line that I have to prove to myself that if I started eating I wouldn't weigh 400 pounds for the rest of my life."

Lucy terminated treatment prematurely but felt satisfied with the progress she had made. She believed that she no longer could deceive herself and no longer felt the need to deceive others.

CHAPTER 5

The Unwilling Patient

ANOREXIC PATIENTS are often unwilling to be in treatment, particularly in psychotherapy. This unwillingness confronts the psychotherapist with a number of contradictory and at times unsolvable problems, including the ethical question of treating a patient without consent. While the situation is somewhat different in each case and needs to be handled individually, some decisions are more clear-cut than others. When a patient is very belligerent and physically is not doing too poorly, the wisest course of action might be to postpone therapy until she is willing to take part in it. The question is more confusing when the patient is in poor health and unable to take care of herself, and where hospitalization is necessary as a life-saving measure. In such cases, I see the patient regularly while she is hospitalized medically, acknowledging that she is a "captive audience" who can refuse to be interviewed. These refusals need to be respected, but I have found that patients often protest but then take part in an interview. This tactic has been a great help in establishing contact with unwilling patients.

Many of the letters of inquiry I receive ask for advice on how to persuade an unwilling patient to come for a consultation. Many patients will finally agree to participate, however reluctantly, when arrangements have been made for a consultation or extended therapy. Yet in some cases opposition to therapy may be so strong that the patients refuse to go near a doctor's office, convinced there is nothing wrong with them, or not feeling that they can trust a physician. Others may permit themselves to be taken to the office but will not participate in the process. One time I saw a fifteen-year-old girl whose parents brought her to the office without mentioning her absolute refusal to cooperate. She proved completely unapproachable, managing to say "I don't know" or "I don't care" more than forty times during the interview. The only question to which she answered with a sentence was "Why did you come if you did not want to talk?" Her answer was "I always obey my parents." I could not use this time for a family session or parent interview because her parents had left the waiting room ("for a cup of coffee") and did not return until the end of the hour. They admitted, when asked, that they had known about their daughter's negative attitude but had expected that a psychiatrist could handle it.

The following cases illustrate the variety of ways patients show their initial unwillingness to participate in treatment.

86

Anna: A Fighting Spirit

A negative, combative attitude does not necessarily mean that no contact can be established. Anna, a seventeen-year-old high school student, was brought for a consultation that she had fought literally "tooth and nail." (The father had fresh bite marks on his forearm.) This fighting spirit had dominated all family interactions for the past two years.

Anna was the youngest child in her family and had been an excellent student. Though overweight through junior high school, she had received more honors and awards than her sisters and brothers together. She had expected a prize at the end of junior high school, but the prize was given to a minority child, a result that the family explained was a sign of political pressure in their community. Anna felt so hurt for having been denied the prize she felt was her due that she withdrew from social activities and ate less and less. Until then she had accepted obesity as part of her makeup; she had felt good about herself and felt recognized and respected for her academic achievements. In this situation, however, she had missed being acknowledged and felt deserted by her mother, whom Anna had expected would put up a fight about the injustice. Contrary to previous experiences with dieting, she stuck to the reduced food intake so rigorously that a year later her weight had dropped from over 200 pounds to 94 pounds. Now family concern was centered on her being too thin.

Anna was taken from one doctor to another, with repeated hospitalizations. The consultation with me had been arranged while she was hospitalized in another state, a situation of which I had not been informed. The weight loss had been frought with much aggression and misinformation. For example, one of the physicians had thoroughly frightened Anna's mother by telling her that Anna would die if she lost another five pounds.

Initially it looked as if Anna was not going to cooperate with one more examination, which she feared was bound to end up with her being forced to gain weight even though she did not want to. I accepted her complaint of forced treatment as valid. Anna's history of enforced medical treatment was so glaring that it was easy to agree with her that she should have been consulted about the various medical examinations. After the main factual events had been enumerated in a family session, I saw Anna alone and inquired in detail what the various procedures had meant to her. I maintained that she had a right to know and to learn something from the various experiences. Unexpectedly she opened up and spoke with much emotion about the constant fighting at home, all to get her to accept another medical procedure.

During the second interview she spoke more freely about the event that had precipitated her social withdrawal and the weight loss, a disappointment that had touched on crucial points in her life. I reminded her that her mother had presented the facts in exactly the same form: "From what she says, it was a great unfairness and hurt to you that you were swindled out of what was justly coming to you." Anna revealed that the real hurt was that her mother did not take it to court or fight the injustice in some other way: "The anger against Mother began when the other mother fought for her child and my mother didn't fight for me." Summarizing the situation, I added that it was unusual that this one disappointment seemed to have ruined her life: "There must have been other things where you didn't get recognition, where you felt let down." I raised the question "Why do you waste your time eating and throwing up? That's the greatest waste of time I can think of."

She agreed: "I never thought of it like that before—I can think of better ways to spend money."

By the end of the second session this girl, who, during her first interview, had refused to talk and was screaming accusations at her parents, was now willing to discuss a treatment plan. She would use the forthcoming vacation period to catch up on the schoolwork she had missed. She also agreed to see a therapist near her hometown. She talked openly about the various doctors her family had consulted, most of whom she did not trust and who had not even talked with her at all. Then she suddenly began to talk about plans for her future, the most cherished of which was to go to medical school and become a doctor. She was aware that she had behaved as if she disliked doctors, "but only some. That's why I want to be a doctor. I want to be one that people can trust."

Helen: The Self-Made Victim

Helen, who was twenty-three years old when her father approached me to accept her for treatment, had an outspoken negative attitude. When Helen was seventeen her weight had dropped from 130 to 110 pounds (her height was five feet eight inches). She went to an eastern college where she felt out of place and became depressed. She saw a psychiatrist for a short time but felt whatever transpired was meaningless to her. Her weight was down to 100 pounds when she returned to her home in the west. She attended a local college but became depressed again and lost still more weight.

During the next two years she was repeatedly hospitalized to improve her nutrition and was in treatment with several psychiatrists at various times. She took pride in the fact that she had lost ten pounds during her first hospitalization and that for the past two years her weight had not risen above 90 pounds. Then she decided to finish her college education in Houston and reluctantly expressed willingness to come for therapy.

However, when she arrived at the end of August she flatly refused to be in treatment. She asked to see me alone, without her mother, who had accompanied her. She stated: "Let me tell you right away that my attitude is very bad, very bad. I do not want to come to you. I know I have a problem, but I'm tired of psychiatrists and hospitals and I can barely bring myself to come to this building and to talk with you. I have just spent seventeen days this month in the hospital. They were trying again to make me gain weight. [I had stipulated that I would consider her for ambulatory treatment only if she maintained her weight above 90 pounds.] I want to get away from the idea of being sick and having to see a psychiatrist. You see, psychiatrists haven't helped me, and I have been at it for four or five years."

When I got a chance to get in a word or two, I explained that the psychiatrists' responsibility was not to make her gain weight: "They can help you with the underlying bad feelings, your worries about your own self; that is the psychiatrist's task. But a psychiatrist cannot work with a starving organism because hunger interferes with the psychological functioning. That is another question—for your nutrition you need a medical doctor." She admitted that she did not feel right about being skinny. "I hope that it is easier for me to eat out here, away from the family."

She added, "But don't tell my mother that I don't want to come. She would flip her wig if she heard me say that I didn't want to come or I didn't think I needed to come, and that I wanted to try to gain weight on my own. I have been doing this for years—go, go, go, and nobody has helped, helped, helped. So I'm tired of it."

I inquired about her previous experiences with psychiatrists and what she had learned about herself. "What did I learn? I don't know what I learned. I didn't have faith in them. I'm sorry, I appreciate you, you're wonderful, but I don't believe you. I get sick of it. I have wasted thousands of dollars."

I explained to her that unless she wanted therapy nothing could be done, but of course I would not tell her mother that she was in treatment when she was not. I suggested that she be seen regularly by an internist. She agreed to this, and I questioned whether it might be of help for her if we set a certain date for her to see me again, perhaps in a month, and report on how well she was doing. An exchange ensued that foreshadowed something characteristic of the whole treatment period, namely, her trapping the other person into making a decision for her. She answered, "If you want to." My reply was "No, would it be of help to *you?*" I commented on her skill at letting other people make decisions for her with which she would comply: "Then you can complain that after all you didn't want it."

Her reply confirmed this. "Of course I don't want to. But if it would make you feel better, sure I will." "See?" I replied. "That's what I mean, you turn it around and you will do it to make me feel better. Will it make *you* feel better?" She answered, "I'll go and see this doctor once a week." I confirmed, "Fine, we'll leave it at that. And you will leave it up to him to tell you when you need to see me. Then you will feel happy because someone else forces you again." At that point she turned to her mother, who had joined the session a few minutes earlier, and said, "Maybe I should make just one appointment.

Is that a good idea, once, just to tell her? But I don't know."
Since the mother did not take a stand she repeated, "Mom, do
you think it is important that I come back in a month and
report? Is that good?" I said, "You say you want to hack it
alone, you want to be unsupervised. That is all right with me."
She then admitted, "Maybe it will make me feel more secure
to know that in a month I will check it again, maybe that would
give me a good feeling."

This little episode correctly foretold things to come. Whatever came up and whatever decision needed to be made, she
would try to have someone else make the decision so she would
be the victim who was being manipulated.

As things turned out, she phoned three weeks later to make
sure that the appointment for the following week still stood.
Now she was eager to talk. "Things are working out fine, but
I'm just not gaining weight. I'm not dating any boys and I'm
still sick. I'm tired of living this way. I'm tired of not wanting
to do anything about it. It sounds so simple, but I just can't
do it. Take, for example, a regular day—I ate breakfast and
then I went all day till ten o'clock at night and I wasn't really
hungry but I wanted to eat. So I sat down and had some French
fries, and when I had six or seven I started saying to myself,
'You are going to gain weight if you eat all of these late at
night.' I left and took the plate with me. I chewed up French
fries and spit them back onto my plate. I wouldn't swallow
them because I knew if I swallowed them I might gain weight.
So I know I'm sick when I do stuff like that. I can't make
myself eat, even if I'm hungry. I'm afraid to gain weight and
then I hate the way I look. I have been stuck at this level for
the past two years and I feel no psychiatrist has been able to
help me. If you help me I'll come. I do not know how often,
because I don't like it—but I have to talk to someone."

She was aware that there were some contradictions in her

statement. "Starving makes me drive too fast and walk too fast," she said. She tried to eat only foods that would not make her gain weight. "I want my body back. But I'm scared of the weight. If anybody said 'You are putting on weight' or even 'You look better,' it would kill me. If you would say it, I would jump right out of this window." She asked rather urgently, "What is the key? What makes it go away?" My answer was "self-respect." I explained that there was no "it" that had to go away, but that she herself needed to develop a more positive attitude about herself and her body.

She picked up the concept of self-respect and explained that she felt that she had never been truly liked by others. This problem became worse in high school. She had played an important role in the extracurricular activities of her school until she became preoccupied with her body and began losing weight. Going to college turned out to be anticlimactic and she became depressed. Her weight dropped from 110 to 100 pounds. Now her weight was much lower. She had had one date this month and went to a movie and dinner. "At the end he said, 'I'll call you,' but he didn't. I'm sure they think I'm weird—so skinny and depressed."

She went on: "Today I wanted to come—I know I need it. I can't snack—I have to be hungry. I eat breakfast and will not put anything into my mouth until dinner. If somebody would just fall in love with me and give me the self-esteem, then I would eat." I would not let this statement pass without correction, that love alone would not do it, that she needed to correct the low opinion she had of herself. She agreed that she took no pride in her self now: "Food has too much significance. It is like a monster standing there waiting to attack me. It says 'I dare you to eat me.' Food speaks to me: 'I'm going to make you fat.'"

She continued: "If you can get me over my hangup you are

a miracle worker. I hashed over all the reasons for all these years—and it doesn't go away." I repeated my previous formulation that there was no "it," but that only she could overcome this illness by changing her attitude and that I would be glad to help her with that task. To this she replied with an honest "Help me," and we then discussed the practical aspects of treatment.

Esther: Clinging to Thinness

In this example, the patient's initial attitude seemed to be exactly the opposite of other negativistic, unwilling patients. Esther was a twenty-four-year-old woman who had had a weight problem since she was about ten years old and had been anorexic for six years. At age fourteen her weight was 140 pounds. Under continuous pressure to reduce, she weighed 110 pounds on graduation from high school. Even before enrolling in an eastern college, Esther became more rigid in her dieting, claiming that she had heard that people would "blow up" on going to college. She weighed 105 pounds when she entered college. Five weeks later she came home and her weight was down to 90 pounds. She was seen by several physicians, who applied various organic diagnoses to her condition.

One of them was outspoken and told her, "You and I know why you have lost all the weight. Have you ever heard about anorexia nervosa?" She was so shocked by his frankness that she refused to go back to him, and her family found another physician who treated her for a liver condition. On discharge he told her mother, "Let her eat anything she wants, do anything she wants, to put that weight back on." "Well, then I went absolutely crazy, had food binges and everything. I think I made like a game out of it. Then, because here it was the first time in my life that I didn't have to worry about calories, I was just eating everything and anything I could possibly get." Esther's mother tried to direct her to eat more wholesome foods than cake and ice cream, but Esther quoted the doctor as having said "Let her eat anything she wants." She explained, "I could have half a coffee cake at one time, along with anything else, and I didn't feel guilty about it either, because I remembered what the doctor had said." The result was that she gained weight very rapidly. "I jumped from 90 pounds and never thought of stopping when I hit 100 pounds. I was 105 one week, and the next thing I knew I was 118, and that's when I stopped weighing myself."

The experience left her not only with the need for reducing again but with a panicky fear of being unable to control her intake when she was not losing weight. After that she did anything and everything to keep her weight at a low level. She was even afraid to follow instructions for a diet that was calculated for a slow weight gain. The next year her weight went down to 105 pounds. At that time she became engaged to a young man whom she had known since her high school days and who, she felt, would understand her. But she hesitated about getting married because the concept of the sex act was unacceptable to her.

She lived in an apartment not too far from her parents' home, took some courses to complete her education, but was most preoccupied with dieting and exercise. She would walk up the ten floors to her apartment. When her weight went down to 80 pounds she was hospitalized for intravenous feeding. She spoke with resentment about having been "blown up" from 80 to 93 pounds during that hospitalization. On discharge her physician arranged for psychiatric treatment, something she had absolutely refused until then.

Although she liked her psychiatrist, not much was accomplished, and he advised her that she needed to be in treatment away from her oppressive home environment. With her doctor's agreement she contacted me and asked for treatment in Houston. In spite of my cautious reply her parents insisted on coming to Houston at once, explaining that her weight was at a life-threatening level (70 pounds). Despite my reluctance, the family appeared at my office and insisted that she be accepted for treatment, praising my skill and reputation.

Esther was admitted to the medical service with the understanding that her nutrition needed to be improved, either by eating regular food or by intravenous feeding. The attending physician felt that Esther could reach a safe weight within three to four weeks. If she then felt well enough to come regularly to therapy, arrangements would be made. If that were not possible, she would need long-range residential treatment, as the referring psychiatrist had suggested.

Esther and her parents were flattering in a coercive way: the parents stated that I was the only person to whose care they could entrust their daughter. I learned little about the background of Esther's anorexia except what I could observe during the interview. The father was detached in a businesslike way, interrupting his wife and daughter when they tried to explain anything. He stated repeatedly that he wanted the opinion of the doctor, who was the expert, and that what they had to contribute did not matter. The mother, in contrast, acted like the well-informed psychotherapist who explained everything and offered her help in therapy. Esther just went along, claiming over and over that she wanted a normal life.

When Esther was admitted to the medical service her

weight was only 69 pounds. She complained endlessly about the quality of the room, the nursing care, the interest of the dietician, and so on. It soon became apparent that Esther talked a great deal about her intention to get well but would not follow the carefully calculated diet. The therapeutic sessions were friendly, but Esther was so circumstantial and evasive that I learned very little about her development except her incredible need to remain dependent.

We planned to keep Esther on the medical service until her weight was in a safe range. Her weight increase was very slow, to just 75 pounds by the Christmas holidays (about six weeks after her admission). Esther was upset about the prospect of her parents' visit. Christmas had always been a big holiday in her family, and Esther felt guilty that they would be disappointed that she had not gained more weight. "I'm just worried that it's going to throw me back eatingwise." I expressed concern that we had learned so little about the anxiety that kept her from eating. She said, "I am just so afraid that if I go out with them to a food situation, I don't know why, but I just couldn't eat in front of them like I have been eating in the hospital." My comment was "That has to do with your feelings toward your parents, and I think we should talk more honestly about that." She replied, "I do not want to give them the satisfaction of seeing me eat, not yet." I stated that we had not talked about her anger and resentment at all. She replied, "Anger and resentment that I have toward them, you mean? I can eat, but I will not give them the satisfaction."

After several requests for more detail about her anger and resentment, Esther made a stammering and painful attempt to explain: "Oh, it's hard to say. I don't know. I couldn't say. Well, if I didn't get my way. But not really. I can't think of anything that really made me angry. In fact, we haven't ever discussed this, about the turmoil, you know, there would be like turmoil and friction, and I hated it. This was when I was much, much younger, and I'd sit at the table, you know, a little girl should be seen and not heard, and I'd sit there politely, and then there would be the discussion about business matters, and then they would start to argue and bicker. I would try to do anything to divert their attention, so I would even do things that were bad, I mean just to divert their attention." She went on for a long time to conveying an atmosphere of turmoil. I commented, "What I hear mainly is a complete disregard for the needs of a child."

During this whole period I received numerous telephone calls from the mother, usually to correct something that Esther had mentioned. In spite of advice to the contrary, Esther had long daily telephone conversations with her mother and would report everything that had been discussed during the therapeutic sessions. I advised the parents, in particular the mother, to seek help in their local community so that they could handle their anxiety better.

After two months of negligible progress, in spite of Esther's constantly talking about how much she ate, intravenous hyperalimentaion was instituted. During the first two weeks there was an appropriate increase in weight, to 88 pounds. She looked decidedly better, was less tense, and spoke for the first time in more realistic terms about her living conditions, how she felt completely at a loss about what to do and how to make decisions. She became increasingly alarmed about the weight gain, and at 90 pounds the gain stopped. As a matter of fact, there was a slight drop, and six weeks later her weight was down to 88 pounds.

At that time, about three and a half months after she had been admitted to the hospital, and with her weight only a few pounds more than when she arrived, I confronted Esther with the fact that we had nothing to offer her. The effort at refeeding had been frustrated, and in her therapy sessions she stuck to the most superficial descriptions, which she then shared with her mother. I recommended admission to a residential treatment center as the only alternative to going home, to the same situation from which she had tried to escape.

She was panicky at the idea of returning home, and for the first time she heeded the recommendation not to discuss her treatment sessions with her mother. She became very active in exploring the background difficulties. Her style of talking changed; she became more direct and expressed honest feelings of despair and resentment. The change was sufficiently impressive that I reconsidered my decision to discharge her, and I suggested that she enter the psychiatric service, to have daytime activities and to continue psychotherapy. She felt so positive about the situation that she even considered taking a job and living on the outside on her own.

Three weeks after the change in her attitude Esther's parents appeared, to complain about her poor progress. They felt a change was indicated. Esther had a serious relapse, she became depressed and lost weight again. However, for the first time she spoke in realistic terms about wanting a normal life: "I never had the opportunity to prove myself. I did when I was younger, but then somehow I felt squelched."

She now talked in detail about the difficulties she felt: "My whole past experience, the way I've been just existing—I haven't been living; I've just been existing from day to day. I think if I felt like I had accomplished something I would feel better about myself. I see that just clinging to the thinness is nothing. Where has it gotten me? Yesterday I felt more normal when I was eating and not making a big deal about it. Today

I had nothing to do afterward, so I was dragging the lunch out because I didn't have anywhere to get off to. Now I want to be stimulated and take an interest in something. Before I was content just to think about the next meal and dream about the food that I had ordered. But now I want it to become just a natural, normal thing for me."

I praised her for having come to the point of recognizing that "thinness doesn't get me anything" and that she had found it out by herself. She went on to say, "But I want a replacement, something that would reassure me. Being thin hasn't made anything out of my life at all; it has destroyed it." I asked, "How come you closed your mind so long to your need to participate in life?" Her explanation was "I was raised with ready-made pleasures. I never had to struggle for anything; it was always made so easy for me. It was always handed to me. If I was having difficulty, I was always able to get the necessary help to make everything as easy as cake. And if the going got rough, I could just quit. I never had confidence in myself; that's something I have always lacked, and I still do. I still have the great fear of failure. Now I want to feel normal; I want to do things normally."

My comment was "But we need to understand what made you postpone it so long. We spoke so often about my puzzlement that you were doing anything and everything to postpone finishing the hospitalization. All I have heard is 'I am afraid of the next step.' And now you sound ready to take the next step. But what went on in your mind when you dragged it out?" She answered, "I guess it wasn't until just the past week that I saw there was something, that there is a life I have a chance to get into." I reminded her that she couldn't get well without looking into the fear of gaining weight. And I reminded her that during the two weeks on the intravenous feeding she had talked about personal things and spoken entirely differently, but when the weight gain stopped she went back to her stereotyped complaining.

The parents meanwhile were exceedingly critical. They removed Esther from the hospital against her wishes and took her home. Several months later she phoned and told me with much pride that things were going better. She had recognized that she would do better if she kept out of her parents' way. She was taking college courses to complete her education and spoke of independent activities.

Fawn: Living on Air

Fawn, a thirty-year-old woman who had been anorexic for eight years, expressed her negative attitude toward psychotherapy strongly. Though polite, she appeared completely uninterested in what was discussed, exhibiting a superiority with condescending criticism. She had maintained an active life until her weight had declined to about 60 pounds, which was very low for her height of five feet nine inches. Progressive ill health had forced her to give up her independent life abroad. She had spent the last few months in a medical hospital without improvement. Psychiatric treatment had been urgently advised but she refused it. Fawn's father, an eastern industrialist, came to Houston for a consultation and made arrangements to bring his daughter for treatment.

Many anorexics approach life and relationships, and therefore also the therapist, with an attitude of "I have no rights, but I have to please other people." This was probably most pronounced in Fawn's case. She strongly objected to psychiatric treatment but added, "If that's what Daddy wants, that is what I'll do." She disowned her own interest by explaining that she did it only for her father's sake. I attempted to make her not only realize but also accept that she was in treatment for her own sake, not to please Father or her internist or even me.

This young woman not only looked like she was starved, she was so weak that she was barely able to walk and needed support. I summarized for her the information her father had given me two weeks earlier: "You are the oldest daughter, and I hope it doesn't sound unkind if I repeat that your father felt that your mother tried to overcontrol you, that there was too much pressure. Is that correct? Yes—and that you seemed to have a hard time getting a feeling of satisfaction from what you were doing, that Mother's doubting attitude had interfered. Father told me the externals. What you and I should discuss are the inner problems—how can a young woman who has been overdominated by her mother find a sense of worthwhile identity?" Her response was polite but negative: "I don't feel insignificant as far as I am concerned." As it turned out, she had read widely on anorexia nervosa, and she immediately rejected any implication that she was "like your anorexics" or that she suffered from low self-esteem.

I tried to get information on the outer constellation of the family, her education and efforts at careers, but she was very reluctant to say anything about her parents or to give any details about her own life. She became even more reluctant when I asked about the development of her illness and the weight loss. "I don't fit into that category [anorexia nervosa] except that I come from a wealthy family. Yes, but that's all." I agreed that there was a name for this illness but that it was not an illness of weight and dieting. "This is an illness of inner self-awareness, of inner feelings of relatedness, and of feelings of fulfillment. The real problem isn't the weight and food; the problem is in the sense of inner worthwhileness and well-being. From the few things that you have said I have gained the impression that you have worked on these things." Her response was "Doctor, I'm a bright young woman. My problem is that I know so much, and I can't see where you fit in. I know a hell of a lot, and I'm not just saying that. I'm not a stupid chicken."

At that point I interrupted and asked, "Who has treated you like a stupid chicken?" She rejected the notion, saying, "I don't mean that literally. I don't mean that at all. I'm not saying anybody did. I just know more than most people in most situations but I don't believe in psychiatry. Therefore, why not say so?" I commented that she had difficulty applying her knowledge to herself. She interrupted me: "—But I don't want to be rude." She again protested against perceived coercion to fit herself into one particular category, explaining that she did not want to be a clone or a specimen of her social class but wanted to take part in life in her own way. I repeated my comment: "There must be something bothering you because you are in, if nothing else, an unusually weak condition." She responded, "Yes, Doctor, but that is getting better. I have always done everything for myself. As a child I got in trouble if I said what I believed. Then I got to a point where I knew more than a lot of people. I don't mean that unkindly—I don't mean to sound like knowing it all."

I followed this up with an explanation that often young children are much brighter and more observant than adults give them credit for. It seems that she had been one of these very bright, observing children who drew conclusions that were all right in the childhood perspective but then lead to difficulties later on. This time she agreed: "It's just that there wasn't any fairness. It just wasn't fair. I don't mean that now, but that's how I saw it when I was a child. It was not fair. Now I have chosen the life I live." I added here, "But you have chosen a way of life that is rather painful and exhausting." She interrupted, "If you forgive me, I think that's not exactly accurate. Is it all right if I correct you?" To which I answered, "By all means. I make a tentative guess and I expect you to correct it or enlarge it."

She continued: "Sometimes it feels a little bit nice to speak about the pains, because it wasn't fair as a little girl. There wasn't any way of winning. You were wrong before you started." I asked for further explanation, because her father had not gone into details. "Oh, he doesn't know. Daddy did the best he could; Mommy did the best she could. They're both trying to live, just like I'm trying to live. I really don't blame them for anything. They're doing the best they know how." I agreed with this but at the same time explained that a little child experiences being misunderstood and having to give in as painful unfairness. She took up the word "misunderstood." "My goodness, eventually I just didn't say anything. You wouldn't be accepted from what you said, or you'd be wrong and then you could be forced."

She talked in more detail about the inconsistencies in her early life and added, "They have been so kind to all of us. And that is not a little kid speaking who is repressed and scared to say anything. I think one of the major things to get past is feeling like I'm considered the selfish, ungrateful child who runs all over the world, who is a spendthrift; who doesn't understand about money, doesn't understand about anything. I need understanding and softness, and my father understands this more than my mother. But I want him to understand also that I didn't want to come to see you because, you know, all this talking, talking all the time, spilling all these tales, means nothing to me. If it means something to Daddy, that's a difference. And that brings up the classic theory of 'Oh, she has to please her parents.' It is not like that. More and more I begin to realize that I can say what I think. I went to school and didn't even know that you could dislike a course. It never occurred to me until I had to choose my courses in the freshman year in college."

She alternated such informative statements with complete denial of needing to be in treatment. She introduced each disagreeing statement with "I don't mean to be rude—" to which I responded after a while, "What puzzles me, even concerns me, is that you are continually so apologetic." She replied, "That's my way." And I enlarged: "How were you raised to be so apologetic? You keep repeating 'I don't want to be rude.' Please understand that I want to hear what you truly feel, and I respect it and do not sit here with criticism but accept it." That was one of the few moments when she truly agreed, that she had never felt accepted. She explained further how she felt as a child, even more as an adolescent, that she was malleable in a certain way.

The whole session went in this up-and-down of her giving some information but then denying it. She reported that her mother had been sick the previous week and that she had phoned her and honestly asked, "Is there something I can do for you?" Her mother responded, "Well, yes, just get yourself well, that's what the whole family is waiting for." I used this opportunity to make a strong statement. Getting well for her family would be the opposite of what we were after. She could recover only for her *own* sense of what was right for her. I pointed out that on the other hand, "this extreme thinness, and I've seen it in others, is like a desperate cry for help: 'Please pay attention to my inner needs.' " To this she replied, "Please don't put me into the class with anorexics—please." Through several weeks she maintained this role of a helpless, pleading, submissive patient, constantly expressing, "How can I please you?" Yet at the same time she was quite grandiose in her sense of reality and very demanding in what she wanted.

She was admitted to the medical service for refeeding. We spent a few days observing what she ate, and it was so little that intravenous hyperalimentation was decided upon. In spite of some initial difficulties she cooperated well with this plan and gained thirty pounds in three months. After she had gained about ten pounds she was allowed out of bed, and she walked all over the hospital with the feeding stand behind her. She spent most of her time in the cafeteria, where she established in one corner something like a home office. She maintained an active correspondence with friends and colleagues and became increasingly interested in reestablishing her old activities. During this time I saw her regularly in psychotherapy. The intravenous feeding apparatus precluded her coming to my office, and I went to see her in her room, or later in the cafeteria. She and I agreed that she was a "captive audience," but a lot of ground was covered. She maintained the basic attitude that she saw me only to please her father, but she was always eager to talk.

Things became more lively when she was off the intravenous feeding but still hospitalized. As long as she was attached to the machine she was rather vague about what she ate. Off intravenous feeding, she expressed herself more freely about food and in other areas as well. One day the conversation drifted to dresses and how to select them. Since she usually wore her bathrobe, seeing her beautifully dressed was a surprise. She discussed it, comparing the choice of a dress with the selection of a sculpture. "If I were to buy one . . . Goodness, do you think

I'll have a body and everything else and move through the world in a way that satisfies me without having to pamper?" I commented on her having such a positive, accepting attitude toward her body: "But it doesn't explain why you have denied yourself the basic human right of staying healthy." She objected that I really could not understand her: "I don't think you are going to be able to make the connection between the way I basically am and the way I was." I responded, "I am glad to hear that because that is exactly what I have felt, that there is a lot to be filled in. It may be exactly what I have been talking about, why I have kept on asking the same question, namely, 'What is missing, what is lacking?' After all, you are the same person who arrived here three months ago and could scarcely drag herself around and who was, you may recall it, anxious and tense and frightened. And now we can talk about it. And you say I haven't made the connection. Is that correct? I try to understand the continuity. You say it is so different that I can't possibly see it."

Fawn hesitated but then said, "Perhaps I could just say a couple of things that come to me out of context, and I ask if you'll be nice enough please not to try to relate them back or paint them in." I answered, "I won't throw them back at you. Whether I link them up I can't promise; I have to follow the way my mind works."

She enlarged a great deal on what she would like to say, and it became apparent that her great fear was to be laughed at. She asked me to "please do not take lightly what I think I am going to say now. Nor will you try to thread it together, perhaps very quickly. Because I don't think it is simply a matter of putting things together." I promised her that I would not make premature connections, but that on the other hand if one gets only spotty information it would be merely human to try to put it together to make it plausible: "The more real information I have, the easier it is to drop the effort to combine them, and getting the real information is what matters." It became apparent that her other concern was that I would think she was suicidal when she spoke in metaphysical terms about this life and how it differs from experiences in the past. I made a serious effort to follow her reasoning but was honest in saying when I was no longer able to follow.

She attempted to clarify in an impersonal intellectual manner: "One would like to learn how to communicate one's lesser anxieties to others when one is pushed past a certain dimension of mysteriousness. Then where does one make a push outward onto what at a certain time? That's what I mean; it's going to get so tangly that it is not at all clear—not tangly for me, but tangly for you." I reminded her that that morning she had given me an excellent definition of what she felt therapy could do, namely, that she was using me to reexamine her own issues and thinking that she was doing the work. I added, "Another thing that is goes on in therapy is that communication is used to establish mutual understanding. Your saying 'It must sound tangly to you' is correct. Therefore our goal is to put it into simpler words so that I can follow what you are saying."

Although she objected when I tried to interpret that she seemed to have a dreadful fear of being cast into a mold, she explained, "What I'm trying to say is that there is something about which most people seem to be most anxious in their life but where there does not exist any anxiety for me. I'm just saying that most people are disturbed about dying and I'm not." I reminded her that this was similar to what she had said before and that I did not believe her behavior was suicidal. I added, "You have convinced me that what you were doing to your body was not a death wish, it was nearly the opposite. But you had endangered your life."

She was definite: "Well, it clearly wasn't intentional. To end up in the state I was in, that was nuts. In addition, it was a little different from that. I am really very disciplined, and if I believe in something I really work hard at it. How much, how much I enjoy the streamlinedness of it, the simplicity. I really care about that. But I couldn't stay alive. My 'less is more' sort of thing, and also wishing to feel the consciousness of my body. So the coupling of a variety of things made me arrive at this very, very streamlined diet in which there clearly wasn't sufficient nutrition to sustain life."

About two weeks after the intravenous feeding was discontinued Fawn left the hospital and stayed for the next few weeks with friends of her family. She came to her sessions quite regularly. The therapeutic sessions during that time were seemingly arguments in which she reproached me for not understanding her, for exaggerating things, for making her talk about things that were better forgotten. The main theme that appeared over and over was illustrated by her statement that, after all, she had not chosen to be my patient.

She had gone to the trouble of returning from a trip in time for her appointment but then began the session with the declaration: "I am not going to talk to you any more. After all, I am here to see you only because I promised my father. Now, of course, if you run to him and complain about me, then everything is lost." She added, "Of course, I try so hard to tell you what you want to hear." To this I replied as I had many times before: "Don't forget, the goal isn't to make me feel good, the goal is to make you feel more independent." After some more exchange I added, "This session is all right, because you are talking honestly about what you feel and that you are upset." Her response was "The upset is over coming here. It isn't you. It is that I am tired of coming here, and that is why I am upset." In spite of her repeated declaration that she was not going to talk to me any more, in this session she talked more than at probably any other time. She was much more personal and direct in attacking me, even using swear words, something she had never done before. She went into a detailed explanation: "See, that is what disturbs me here. I say one thing, and you and the authority figures will say that it means so and so. I have just gotten tired of saying what I feel. I think you are not going to accept it, I am tired of it. That's what it was like when I was a little girl."

The main theme of that session was that she could not talk to me because I might raise questions, and questions meant criticism, and criticism in turn meant not being accepted, the way she had felt as a child. In the beginning of treatment, Fawn had declared that certain things would never be discussed, and one of these forbidden topics was her mother. From the first day on she had said, "I will never talk about my mother. She is a lovely lady—it so happens we didn't get along. I will never mention her." I had to admit that I knew very little about her mother. But in this session Fawn went on to say for the first and only time that I looked like her mother, that I acted like her and behaved like her. For more than a few minutes it sounded as if she truly saw in me the picture of her mother. "If you would just hear, Dr. Bruch, when I say something that really matters to me, but then you explain it and make me feel that I'm not right. I know you mean to be honest, but it is a repeat problem from my childhood." This was the one and only time she said, "This is just the way it was when I was a child, and you are like my mother and you are doing exactly the things she did—whatever I say, you disagree and you discourage me. You belittle me, and you look and act like her." That was a very strong emotional reaction, the most she expressed during the short period of treatment. The recurrent theme was that my not agreeing with her was criticizing her, condemning her the way her mother had always condemned her.

What were the things I disagreed with? Fawn was convinced that some people could live on air. She had tried that but had become convinced that for her it did not work. She was still convinced, however, that there were people who could live on air, and they were superior people. I had disagreed with her on this point and also on the point that she could get well without gaining weight. Psychologically she was most evasive. But when I used a word like "evasive" or "denying," that was criticism. She felt she needed to be praised and accepted for her opinions.

In the session where she saw me as her mother, she became more emotional and began crying. When we discussed the next appointment she came up with her old statement, "I come here only because Daddy says so." When I made a concrete suggestion about the next appointment she answered, "You see, the thing is to keep you satisfied and for me to express myself emotionally. What happens if next time I don't desire to cry? Do I have to fake the crying for you to be complimented or for you to be satisfied?" This was partly a serious question, but there was also an intentional teasing or putting me down.

While Fawn maintained her weight and seemed to accept the need for definite physical nutrition, she became concerned with something she called "nextness." She attempted to explain: "Nextness is about my life. Not the way it was before. There is still a tremendous commitment to my work, but there is very much less fear that my life will run out."

I summarized my observations about her concept about "nextness." She always had given the feeling of a very limited time, that she was always rushed about what was going to happen, "whereas when you talk now there is a matter-of-fact continuity of planning, of thinking, of living." She added, "And something else that pleases me very much: I feel stronger about my life and my work and about me, that if something goes haywire with plans it's sort of okay. I mean, there is then something else that can take its place. The center of me is my work, and I am convinced of the possibility and the breadth of the ramifications of that work. And there are people who are connected with the work and people with whom I can be friends."

She talked not only about the friends abroad but also about a better relationship to her home. I interpreted her difficulties with family relationships: "In an indirect way you have been telling us that you have been concerned about how to please Mother without being dominated." She spoke now in a more direct way, without denying first what she was going to say or what she had just said. She explained how the lives of people in her family were filled with a lot of curious problems and that she felt less involved with them now. She talked now about the range of possibilities and choices that she had in living with her family and with friends. She felt she had also worked out how she could handle her eating without getting negatively involved with other people. "I could do it, however, I felt I wanted to at the time. [Here "it" likely refers to living her life rather than just eating.] I don't think now so much that I would feel as though I *ought* to. It's like, I like what *I* like." To reinforce this statement, I reminded her that I had been so persistent in saying that I did not feel she could benefit from treatment if she did it for her father's sake. Treatment had to be something for herself.

In what turned out to be our very last session, I asked Fawn about the next appointment, and she answered, "I'm actually thinking that I may not be here on Wednesday." To my question "You mean today is our last session?" she replied, "I was sort of thinking that it might be, for a while." I expressed feeling contented about the things that had been discussed but added, "There is still so much change going on." Her answer was "Well, I can decide to be back here, but that means coming back." To this I responded, "And we'll have another independent, person-to-person talk—and not to please anybody else. Do you recognize the difference? Do we know how it happened that the change took place?" Her answer was in a different style: "When I began to feel like you were a person and I began to think how it might be constructive. Then it was me thinking how it could be constructive, distinct from you as an authority figure or pleasing Daddy or whatever." It was on this note that we terminated treatment, at least for the time being, with her feeling that she was an active participant who accepted that she was doing things for her own sake.

These few examples suffice to illustrate that in spite of a patient's negative attitude, good therapeutic communication can be established. The attitude toward treatment remains tenuous, and the tendency to interrupt persists. This was particularly striking in Helen as well as Fawn, but their declared unwillingness did not keep them from communicating. During the very first interview, Fawn, in spite of her objections, expressed something that may have been true for many of the patients: "Sometimes it feels a little bit nice to speak about the pain, because it wasn't fair as a little girl."

CHAPTER 6

Disturbed Concepts of Food, Body, and Self

THE OUTSTANDING SYMPTOM in anorexia nervosa is a severe weight loss, so severe that it immediately draws attention to a patient. Various words have been used to describe the anorexic's body: severely emaciated, cachectic, skeletal. The excessive thinness is the outcome of a restricted food intake and/or excessive exercise and activity. The history of a patient usually includes information about this changed behavior. Very often relatives are more insistent than the patients in describing the abnormal starvation intake. The patients are apt to explain that they have no hunger, or that they eat enough, or that they feel full.

Formerly psychotherapy was preoccupied nearly exclusively with unconscious conflicts and motivations, and interpretations aimed at clarifying the unconscious motives. The importance of disturbances in the perceptual and conceptual areas were comparatively neglected. Anorexics misuse the eating function in their effort to solve problems in various areas of living that have nothing to do with nutritional needs. In doing so they suffer from a perceptual flaw in that they are frequently unable to differentiate between hunger and other sensations and feeling states: the brain is continuously making mistakes in its effort to discriminate between bodily and psychological needs.

A special form of disturbed food intake is bingeing, the impulse to eat as much as possible, followed by throwing it up. Anorexics feel a definite sense of achievement in controlling how little they eat. Therefore, they may claim that they were introduced to this uncontrolled overstuffing with food by others and may hold these people responsible for the habit. More recently, with all the publicity about bulimia, patients say they read about it in the newspaper or saw it on television. If a patient limits herself to compulsive eating without vomiting, then there will be weight increase, to the point of obesity. This is rare now. Most anorexics who binge handle it in a different way: they will feast, vomit, starve, and feast again. When no place is available to vomit in privacy, they will return to the rigid food control and starve for a few days. They run into such situations when visiting with friends or family, or on a skiing or sailing weekend, or something along that line. When they cannot throw up, they just do not eat.

This type of excessive eating followed by vomiting has been known to occur in otherwise classic anorexic patients. The syndrome of overeating and vomiting appears to have become much more frequent. In my own observations, it has more than doubled. Among the patients described in *Eating Disorders,* binge eating occurred in about 25 percent of the cases. In recent years it occurs in at least 50 percent of the cases. Whether or not, or how, bulimia is related to true anorexia nervosa is not quite clear. There is a tendency to label every young girl who overeats and vomits an anorexic or, by a semantic atrocity, "bulimarexic," as if the conditions were the same. There were always anorexics who would overeat and vomit but who would stay, in their overall behavior, in the anorexic state. While the binge-purge cycle may occur during the first or second year of the anorexic illness, often it appears later. When the simple starving becomes too strenuous or exhausting, then the idea of eating and vomiting looks like a solution, in order for the patients to give in to their desire for food and to stay slim at the same time. Usually the initial weight loss in patients whose primary eating disturbance is bingeing and purging is small, but it may become more severe as patients develop a feeling of not being in control.

As time goes on, these patients make repeated efforts to stop or cut down on the binge eating, but usually give up after a few days. Gradually the eating binges get separated from mealtime or desire for food, and become more and more a response to emotional upset or disappointments. Some do it on a time basis; whenever there is unplanned time, a "void," they fill it with eating. In others it becomes "just a habit." For still others years of addiction to the practice ensue: "Well, it has gone away on several occasions for about four days to a week, because I felt really good for that length of time for one reason or another, mainly external reasons." But if this good feeling does not continue, bingeing recurs full force.

A woman of nearly thirty who had binged and vomited for

ten years explained, "I know it is something I could control, but I know that it is hard, so hard. It is like a drug addiction to give up without help. When I'm feeling really happy, it is so easy to stop it for a day or two. It is something I do, but I have no desire to do it when I'm feeling well. I also have very little desire to do it when I'm feeling really upset. When I'm feeling really terribly upset for a particular reason, I do it, but I have to force myself to do it, I don't really want to."

She also compared it to behavior observed in connection with chain-smoking, "like someone who knows she shouldn't be smoking and knows it is bad for her, but who goes through the seconds and minutes and hours, day by day, resisting it, and then finds it overwhelming. It is so overwhelmingly hard that I almost plan to do it. When I start thinking at the beginning of the day that I'm not going to throw up that day, I throw up real early in the day, usually because thinking of the resistance, the resistance even being pictured in my mind, just becomes unbearable. It is sort of overpowering and I stop thinking of other things. All I think is how I'm going to be able to resist." She described how she felt becalmed after having gone through the ritual; her conviction that it works for her as a sedative becomes stronger with each repetition. Her way of handling the desire to binge and vomit is just to give in instead of being tense all day over how to control the impulse.

Many patients find that the best way is to decide to throw up as the last thing in the day. When this is planned, they do not need to worry. But if they decide *not* to throw up, "then I start worrying, and the worrying is just exhausting, and I start thinking, 'God, it is just not worth the effort,' and I just go ahead and do it. Then I don't feel anxious about it anymore."

Bingeing used to be a symptom about which patients kept very quiet. Some stopped treatment rather than tell about their great secret of filling themselves up and vomiting. In the last few years, however, bingeing has become more or less an accepted symptom, with or without anorexia, and patients are apt to talk about it more openly, if not boastingly.

A woman of thirty-two who had been anorexic for ten years had twice terminated therapy to protect her secret. Now she describes with a certain relish how she goes at seven in the morning to a grocery store that serves a lavish breakfast. When I mention, "But this doesn't sound like much of a binge to me," she adds reassuringly, "But it continues. I haven't told you the whole day yet. Then I buy a dozen doughnuts, because they have a certain kind of doughnut that I like. And I buy whatever I feel like eating—usually some bread, mayonnaise and eggs to make egg sandwiches, and some cookies, a package of Fritos, and so on." She takes all this home and eats a dozen eggs during the morning. After finishing the eggs, "I'll make some sandwiches with mayonnaise and just eat them plain or with just anything I happen to see." She fills her morning with these rituals. "I never let a binge go past two hours, because I'm afraid I'll gain weight. Then I make myself throw up. It's been four years now that I have been doing this regularly, and in the course of those four years I used to gag myself but now I do it without gagging myself. It's kind of a reverse swallow. It's as easy as swallowing, almost."

When details are discussed, it becomes apparent that for a fairly long time these individuals consider bingeing and purging a superior method of weight control. Only in recent years, with the increasing publicity about bulimia, have many patients become aware of the fact that purging is dangerous. Anorexics who eventually die of heart failure due to anorexia frequently have used vomiting or laxative abuse for weight control.

Whether they are engaged in the binge-purge cycle or not, anorexic patients vary a great deal in the significance they attribute to their food intake. They may call it regular eating or may show a seemingly complete lack of interest in the subject. Some are constantly preoccupied with thoughts of food and eating and will talk about it incessantly, whereas others barely mention it and still others will flatly refuse to talk about it. The following cases provide a few examples of the different ways anorexic patients, with more or less severe weight loss, will talk about hunger, their interest in food, their body distortions, and how issues are ultimately tied to their disturbed self-concepts.

Annette: A House Divided

It was difficult to obtain information about what and how and when Annette ate. During much of our contact, as noted in chapter 4, there was a kind of double-track communication. On one level she would say—and she maintained this practically throughout the whole treatment period—that she knew she was too thin and that she wanted to gain weight and therefore would eat. Yet on another level, when efforts were made to learn details about her eating habits, or when her internist tried to give her instruction, she would coolly say, "I know what a good diet is and what I'm supposed to eat—and I shall do it now."

In the course of therapy Annette had gained much greater freedom in exploring personal relationships and her role in their development. However, she remained reluctant to talk about her body, her feelings, and her reactions to it and to bodies in general: "I was always shy in reference to my own body—when I was twelve I felt uncomfortable talking about menstruation or having to shave under the arms. Everything was embarrassing, and when I had to do things with the body I was extremely uncomfortable." She recalls that when she was quite young she was not concerned about her body and would wander in and out of her parents' bedroom. Feelings of embarrassment began long before puberty, however, and they remained fixed to her body. She believed that her entire family was uncomfortable with their bodies. When asked if she had noticed the budding puberty of her older sisters, Annette answered with a certain sarcasm, "I never noticed it—no one went around naked in our home. That's what happened in the home of my friend. I saw her brother one day in the nude and I was mortified. I never have known such a casual acceptance of the body. At home we all were embarrassed."

She always had disliked fat bodies, in particular those of old women with sagging flesh and skin folds. "I always feared being compared to a female body like that. I want to avoid curves—I always avoided looking like a woman." I reminded her that she always was concerned about the future. For example, she did not eat lunch because of a fear of not being hungry enough for dinner. Now she did not want to have a feminine body with curves in order to avoid being a sagging old woman. She corrected me: "Not even that. Even the body of a young woman is something I don't like. The way the female body is built, it has pads in places that do look like bulges. Even right now I think young female bodies are too fat. . . . Last night I thought about really *not* wanting to gain—I do not want to have the kind of body females have. From childhood on I had a negative association, felt it was not nice to look like a woman." She feared and worried about having a midriff bulge. "I always felt,

'I do not want to look like that, bulged, drooping breasts, flabby behind'—it's just not pretty, and that's what I'm trying to avoid." I stated, "That means you are in disagreement with Nature. You believe breasts, stomach, hips are ugly, and that something is wrong with the normal female body. You are in disagreement with the budding of puberty."

Much of the talk about her attitude about bodies came up when her weight had slipped back to 86 pounds and the question of rehospitalization was discussed. Since she had to gain weight in order to stay out of the hospital, Annette felt under pressure and admitted for the first time that she did not want to gain weight. During the whole first year of treatment she had continually spoken about wanting to gain weight but being unable to do it. "I want to have my bones covered but not round here (abdomen and hips). Only the bones on top should be covered, but I don't like it looking like this. It seems that the body changes when a girl grows up. I know that is the way the body is built, but I don't like it." I again commented that there was something more basic involved, a deep conflict with Nature, and not only for one or another feature—there was a conviction that Nature had made a mistake. She gave her picture: "No, things are in the wrong places—there are people with flat stomachs, and that is what I'm striving for, but I'm not built that way. My stomach is my Achilles heel. I'm stuck with it. It is admitting something that I have avoided thus far, that it is an inevitable fact—I cannot avoid, I cannot overcome it." I suggested, "Why not accept normal, healthy woman-hood? You spoke before about being disloyal to old convictions. What do you really have to give up in order to get well?" She answered with vigor, "I have been saying *no* a long time. Academically I have been able to achieve what I have set out to do. I was convinced I could do it with my weight as well."

To calm her down I said quietly, "You can't argue with Mother Nature—" and she finished the sentence, "But I have been doing exactly that. I have been thinking . . . now I'm having to face the fact—I have to accept it—looking like what I don't want to look like." I reminded her that her acceptance of the facts of nature was doing what everybody else has done. "Every girl matures, and you cannot deny it." She protested, "But she does it in the way I don't like." I pointed out that this was the same type of childhood misconception as the fear of being "spoiled" that had dominated her life. Her task now was to give up childish thinking and resistance. She added, "I know—not wanting to mature as a female body is a child's way of looking at it. I never wanted to grow up. I always felt I was a child and would stay with my parents."

Toward the end of her first treatment year she had an upsetting experience. She had dated a young man for a while, and he suddenly told her that he wanted to break up. This was a painful shock, but it forced her to look at herself more realistically. "I cannot go on living like a house divided, being mature and full of achievement 'above the neck' but remaining childish and immature 'below the neck.'" This was the first reference to herself as immature. She felt she gave the impression of being much younger, having the body of an undeveloped twelve-year-old girl. She expressed the wish for help to attain biological maturity, and she was aware of the significance that this was now her own decision.

Her internist discussed with her how to achieve a certain weight gain without the eating going out of control. For the first time she truly listened to what he had to say without silently thinking "I won't do it."

Annette shared an apartment with a roommate, but with separate cooking arrangements, and said she ate one fairly large meal at night, no breakfast or lunch. She maintained her weight for the second year in treatment at above 90 pounds. During our sessions she stated repeatedly that she could not gain, that her body did not accept weight gain, and that people had the image of her as a slim person. When she had become aware that she "did not want to gain" rather than she "could not gain," as she had maintained, she was surprised that her weight did increase when she began eating more. Until then she could say "I want to gain" because she felt sure her body would not accept more weight.

Annette's attempts to follow her internist's suggestions and gain weight were not without difficulty. When the internist suggested a certain dietary supplement sold in drugstores, she figured out that it would be cheaper to buy prepared breakfast food at the supermarket. While studying what was on the shelves, she noticed that the cheapest way would be to buy a carton with twelve separate packages in assorted flavors, most of which she did not like. Single packages in flavors she liked were also available, although the price was slightly higher. She could not bring herself to spend more money just to indulge herself and left the supermarket without making a purchase. To Annette, the thought of buying single packages of the flavor she liked upset her and produced severe guilt for the indulgence of spending extra money on herself, and she ended up buying nothing at all. Then she became angry with herself because she had to make another shopping trip to force herself to buy the single packages while disregarding the fact that they were more expensive.

Even during her recovery this attitude of stinginess was a great handicap to Annette. Even when she "wanted" to gain, her own stinginess, her frightened refusal to indulge herself in any way, interfered with her desire to gain weight. She clung to the need not to appear spoiled and would not permit herself to buy anything but the cheapest brand of any food, nor would she prepare fresh food when there were any leftovers. She would spend hours in comparative shopping, to find a brand cheaper than the one in a more accessible store. To make things convenient for herself, to eat more interesting or tasty food, would be "spoiling herself" and thus violate a basic childhood rule.

The fear of presenting a "spoiled" image resulted in an extraordinarily stingy attitude toward herself that permeated many areas of life—including food. Annette was modest in the way she dressed, though she had daydreams of being dressed with elegance and striking style. She had always been rather frugal in what she permitted herself to eat and always felt uneasy about "eating for pleasure." This stringent attitude toward food had developed long before the actual weight loss.

At one point, while she discussed her conflicting feelings about wanting yet not wanting to gain weight, an expression slipped out that she had never used before: "The little man won't let me." When I called attention to this she became more lively and described that she had the feeling that inside— she could not say where, somewhere in the abdominal or lower chest region—there was a little person, like a child, who protested violently whenever she did something for her own comfort. With encouragement she talked in more detail about this little person who was like she saw herself as a child, the way she never had been, namely, stamping her foot and hammering with her arms in protest, expressing all the anger she had never expressed. We discussed how this fit into her anorexic illness and how the little man was the expression of a childhood that was not finished, because there had never been open and free self-expression. She talked more about "the little man inside me who says 'No!' ": "The little man expresses resistance on a wider scale, a silent, inner, unspoken resistance. This resistance should not be spoken aloud because it is childish and wrong and against what they say, but it gives me reinforcement and a secret satisfaction. I feel pride because I really won out. After all, I fooled the grown-ups."

She talked about the emotional reactions connected to weight changes: "There is so much pride and patting myself on the back—all secret, of course—when I go on the scale and I haven't gained. There is consternation when I do gain weight, especially when I didn't want to and haven't tried. My little man has been tricked and double-crossed. All this is reminiscent of how I felt as a child when I had to go along with the adults because they are right and strong and big."

Talk about bodies frequently resulted in Annette comparing female to male bodies and finding female bodies inferior. She spoke about wanting to be equal to a man, wanting to have the same stamina, "and I want to stay slender because I look more like a man. I push myself to do as much as any man can do. It's more difficult to be with a woman who is strong and efficient, and I can't admit that I am not as strong as she is. It's easy to admit this to a man."

Over time it became more and more apparent that somewhere Annette had a concept of being an independent, self-assertive individual with a definite feeling of self, but she could not reconcile this with her concept of being female, which was that of a nearly slavelike creature. She had turned herself into a caricature of an obedient good girl who had clung to "the rules" even if they had been surpassed by new ones.

When I suggested, "We should examine why you still cling to this illogical conclusion that you must be an obedient good girl," she responded, "But how can I say it is illogical when I know it is behavior that I myself do?" I pointed out, as I had many times before, that this behavior had developed when she was quite young and could not possibly be useful for the rest of her life. "How would your life have been if you had been born a boy—how do you see yourself?" She responded with a definite "It would have been worse, because I would have the same ghastly peace-minded temperament and that is unacceptable in boys. At least in girls it used to be acceptable, but now it is culturally an unacceptable way of behavior. But I continue to behave like that." She added, "The desire to change is always there, change the body, change the behavior, be a leader, assert yourself, and yet taking one step toward assertion I get scared and say, 'Well, I'm not supposed to be doing that.' "

I tried to define more specifically when the destructive inhibitions took over, when it became a definite "I cut myself off, the good things in life are not for me." After a long silence she came up with a memory she had never mentioned before. She was ten years old, in fifth grade, a year in school she remembered as "bright and smiley. We had a good teacher and it was a pleasant class. What I'm thinking of now is that we were studying ancient Greece in history and we had to write an essay about if you were a boy or girl growing up in Greece, where would you rather grow up—in Sparta or Athens? The boys sort of split: half of them wanted to be Athenians, dudes; half of them wanted to be Spartan soldiers and get out and fight. I remember the teacher saying that every girl in the class except one wanted to be from Athens, and wasn't that interesting. Everyone laughed, but I sort of thought, 'Well, I am unique after all.' I wanted to be a Spartan. That's fifth grade, and that pushes things back quite a little bit."

Annette was definite that she had not been influenced by anybody else. "It was the vision of serving a cause and being noble, being a fighting woman and being tough and able to take care of yourself." To others Sparta might be the epitome of self-denial and being punitive; to her it meant martyrdom. "I wasn't just going to sit around the house and play a harp and learn songs. I was going to work. This was really comparing myself to other girls; it wasn't a competition with boys. I guess at that time I wanted to prove that I was physically stronger than any of the other girls."

She herself was surprised that she had such strong ideas when she was that young and at a time when she remembers herself as a plump little girl, not athletic at all. But the need to prove herself as sacrificing was there, as was the sense of aloneness. "The Spartan society was pretty difficult, sort of like living in Russia. No softness was allowed and no failing was allowed; everybody is on their own, and if they are not good enough they are not allowed to stay, and there would have been no help. That was very much what I sensed and acted on later—that I'm all alone and that nobody supports me."

I agreed that this memory revealed how early she had held the idea of putting restrictions on herself, to deprive the body of its pleasures and drive it to top performance. She added, "In a sense they were asexual. Everybody went out to fight together and everybody did this and everybody did that. So there was a sense of asexuality about it—well, this was a little kid reading a history book." And she repeated her amazement that all this was present more than fifteen years ago. This Spartan ideal foreshadowed her behavior during the anorexic phase when being frugal, "not spoiled," was her outstanding virtue, and she expressed repeatedly her determination to "carry on through thick and thin."

In the course of therapy she had come to realize how truly undesirable her state of excessive thinness was in terms of human contact. Soon after she first discussed how isolated she was, Annette had a dream in which she saw herself as the skeleton-thin anorexic she had been and had never admitted to being. At last she felt real horror looking at this creature; she was unable to believe that she herself could ever have been like that. For the first time she spoke about the utter despair of this time in her life, the terror of being caught in a trap of her own making.

Annette repeated the issue of not feeling human during the course of therapy. I told her that I knew it was a weird feeling, but that many other patients expressed the same fear. Annette admitted, "This was very hard to admit. It is sort of a given that if you don't see yourself or your body as everybody else considers them to be, then you are not really human." I stated that other anorexics, and also overweight people on a strenuous diet, admit to this fear of not being really human. Though many anorexics suffer from it when their weight is very low, they do not seem to be quite aware of it at that time. Annette stated, "Well, I have come to much more awareness of it now that I have this consistent desire to be a person. I almost feel that the way I was with the skinniness, with the whole attitude of not wanting to be a woman or an adult or to have a full figure and all the rest, was related to the body and my perception of it."

Later I asked her about the way she appeared on the island (see chapter 4), and she explained: "Looking at myself on the island, I am still a skinny nonperson. In a way, it doesn't matter if I'm isolated and different. I mean, in that image it is all right that my sister [Josie] is on the bridge, because she is more in touch with humanity that I am. As long as I remain so far away from being an acceptable or accepting compatriot with people in the world, I might as well stay on the island." I took up the theme: "So you did experience your skinniness as a great alienation, that of being different?" Her answer was, "Well, I do now." I explained to her that many other anorexics speak about the underlying despair only after they are nearly well. It is only then that they realize or admit that they had felt dehumanized, not part of the human race, while skinny.

Annette enlarged even more about the image: "It was also that I didn't deserve to approach Josie for a place because I had made myself into this phantom on the island. I have made myself into this uncivilized being, if not a cannibal on the island at least something so out of touch and out of tune with the rest of the world that I needed to be kept isolated on an island."

This led me to question what inner necessity in her development had led to her extreme isolation. She explained, "I think, going back to what I see as the blackest of the black, it is my own possessed desire not to be a person. Acknowledging that anorexia doesn't just happen, it is my own attitude that very strongly said 'I still don't want to be normal.' That attitude is the ultimate in guilt. It really is an active volition." I then referred to *I Never Promised You a Rose Garden*, which was being shown as a film at that time, and commented that it would be hard to say what expressed more inner disturbance, creating a world of fantasy or her having created a different body. I ended the session with the comment, "There can be no promise of a garden of roses, but I can state definitely that it will be easier and more rewarding to live in the real world than staying on the skeleton island."

Ida: Superhuman Strivings

As noted in chapter 4, Ida's brother visited her early in the course of her therapy and stayed for a few days. They spent much time together, but one afternoon Ida became very upset.

Before she left for college she had tampered with her scale so that it would show a higher figure. One day her brother weighed himself on her scale and felt that the figure was too high, as if he were suddenly overweight. During a session he attended while visiting, he described what happened: "I thought the scale was broken. Maybe she had dropped it or something like that. So I changed it back, and she went and rechanged it. Then she weighed herself again and she recognized that she weighed much less than she needed for going on a hiking trip. A very critical situation developed when she realized that she could not go on the trip. She repeated that she hated herself, that she didn't understand how we could love her at all, that she was such a bad person, that she didn't know why we loved her. She repeated it today too, for instance, that she often would like to destroy herself and that she feels she isn't worth anything."

I explained, "That is the real psychiatric issue, this degree of self-hatred, of failure in self-esteem and failure in self-value. Was that what bothered you when you first came to see me? This, of course, is the basic question: How come that a girl growing up under such favorable circumstances fails to develop a sense of meaningful self-value?"

The brother enlarged on this theme: "What I can think of is that she misinterprets the reality in many ways. When she does something good she considers it matter-of-fact, but when she tries to attack areas where she can't be outstanding she considers it lousy, no good, and instead of dedicating herself to the things she is good at, she keeps on battling with things that are not her strengths."

She explained to her brother, who had said that she was not really trying, that she had control over her behavior. He made the point, "If you control yourself so well for going down and down, you should be able to control yourself going up." Her reply was "It just so happens that I have done it twice already and he doesn't know about it. It's been in a very similar situation, that I have eaten my way out. So it is not impossible." What she was referring to was the fact that twice the internist had been on the point of hospitalizing her, "but I ate my way out—I gained weight." She would eat reasonably well for one week and gain weight, which she then immediately lost. In a way, she took pride in outsmarting the physicians by gaining just enough to stay out of the hospital.

The brother commented, "It makes you angry that you think that I consider that you don't try hard enough." She answered passionately, "Because you don't know what it feels like. I know it's not reasonable. That's why I originally came here, when I realized it was just not normal for anyone to have a stronger urge inside to lose weight instead of gaining weight, and that this urge was sufficiently strong to make me have a discipline stronger than most people. Looking at it objectively, I know it wasn't good for me. But you have never had such a drive inside, so you cannot possibly understand that there can be anything that is not so simple, and that I can't control myself. . . . Now I plan to do it a third time, eating myself out of it. But I don't see why I have to continue constantly gaining." I explained, "The low weight is like a camouflage for the underlying real problems. And you cannot solve the real psychiatric problems until you let go of the camouflage." Her reply was an angry "But in the meantime I become a balloon just because of psychiatric problems."

After this she began talking more freely about her original weight loss. She had begun dieting when she felt dissatisfied with her life, not as recognized as she felt her efforts deserved, sometimes ill at ease socially, feeling that the other girls resented her flirtatious behavior though at the same time she was frightened of closer contact with men. The dieting was intended to prove her willpower, but then slowly it got out of hand. "When I started I was not thinking of losing much weight, just a few pounds. I never thought of losing as much as twenty pounds." Actually she had lost nearly fifty pounds.

She spoke in more detail about her European trip, when the weight loss began. When she would go to a restaurant, she wanted to go only to the very best. "Often I would go to small villages that did not have such good restaurants, so instead of eating I would prefer just going walking around the country or sitting quietly in churches and hearing the sound go down the passages and feeling the cool. There is a beautiful cool in those churches, always so beautiful. . . . It proved I could do it, it proved that I was strong." She had heard about other people breaking down and going on eating binges. "I would never let myself go like that, no matter what." Only recently had she felt weak for the first time. Until then she had taken pride in being able to outdo anybody else, that her body was stronger than her sensations.

Ida described the philosophical background of her losing weight: "There was a period when I was very ascetic and I believed the mind should control the body completely. That is what I discovered when I had those three days of not eating, that I could go on perfectly well without eating. I got convinced that the mind could go do anything with the body that it wanted to. And I still think so, now more than ever. The mind also trains the body to be able to be more perceptive or less perceptive. If I have to suffer pain, I should be able with my mind to disconnect this pain from my mind's activity."

Throughout this first year of therapy, Ida had her meals at the college dining room but ate only minimal amounts. She would skip lunch and go swimming instead. Swimming played an important role in her life. As she gained weight, or at times of emotional upset, she increased the number of laps she swam. She felt that with this strenuous exercise her muscles would develop so well that the fat would be distributed all over her body and not collect in undesirable places. As a child she had been praised for being athletic and having such well-developed muscles.

She stayed preoccupied with her weight for quite some time. Each time she went home for holidays and short vacations, she would gain four or five pounds, which she would set out to lose, although she did not always succeed. When she reached 90 pounds, she finally admitted that she felt better with her higher weight and enjoyed swimming more. She had continued to swim when her weight was very low, though she turned blue and was absolutely miserable and cold.

As time went on, it became apparent that the anorexic illness served certain functions. Ida felt that it was showing her the road to salvation, that through superhuman discipline she would fulfill her secret hope, namely, getting a glimpse into the world beyond: "The more weight I lost, the more I became convinced that I was on the right way. I wanted to learn to know what was beyond the ordinary living, what happens in the afterlife. Abstinence was just in preparation for special revelations; it was like the things the saints and mystics had done. I also wanted to be praised for being special, and I wanted to be held in awe for doing what I was doing. I found out that it was hard to be recognized by other people as an enlightened person." It was for these reasons that she became so infuriated when people tried to make her eat, and she felt guilty when she broke down and did eat because it would delay her attainment of this special goal. It became more and more

133

difficult to get along with others. "I didn't want anybody to know it, but I was convinced that one day I would get the mystical insight—I was waiting for the day of the great Revelation." From contact with other anorexics she later learned that they all expect something special as reward for their starving. Though each patient expects something different, it is always something superhuman. Only when Ida realized that this hope was not being fulfilled had she agreed to come for therapy. "It is like the pot of gold at the end of the rainbow, only there is no pot of gold," she stated. "There is no merit in going hungry, and you cannot change life this way."

Though talking about her secret expectations helped her to become somewhat more spontaneous, she clung for a long time to the overdiscipline. "You become committed to the way of discipline. I cannot conceive of myself ever living without special discipline. Once you have done it the overcontrolling mechanism condemns you to do it for the rest of your life—at least until the body functions normally." Here I commented, "You turn it around. As long as you exercise this discipline over your body it cannot function normally. I know of your pride in your special discipline, the endless repetition of sacrifice in order to maintain this special pride. Nobody can force you to give it up, but as long as you glory in doing something that nobody else can do, you will have to suffer the consequences. As long as you collect admiration and recognition for doing it you are not ready to give it up."

She answered with much feeling, "It's something I have built up and it has turned out the way I wanted it. This was my choice, and you don't like to give up the one area where you did accomplish what you wanted." I pointed out to her that I saw it as a choice of desperation. She had tried to make her own body an object of her will, "your own kingdom, where you are the tyrant, the absolute dictator." One could only speculate about the despair that made her do this, and she could not liberate herself from it until she understood and corrected the reason for the despair. Her main handicap was her refusal to recognize the positive aspects of her existence; her rigid control indicated the degree of her despair. That her body became the target of this discipline showed how desperately she feared never to achieve psychological freedom.

Gradually she reexamined her compulsion to be outstanding: "Some time ago I saw what a 'not special' life implies—it implies that I don't need to do such hard work. I have humanized work. Ordinary people are not trapped because they are not brilliant in everything." I agreed: "That was the secret of being special. It was the alternative to the fear of worthlessness." She went on: "I noticed that ordinary people are more happy and carefree. To me, 'good enough' was condemnation instead of the state of satisfaction." To help her continue this theme, I summarized her progress thus far: "You begin to consider a total picture of yourself, no longer isolated symptoms. I am so glad this change finally took place. As long as there was mistrust this whole illness was the extreme of self-sufficiency—the less you let into your body, the better off." She took up this theme: "But self-sufficiency out of fear, not out of strength. Now that my confidence has increased I feel the strength. I still consider it a crime not to develop one's potential." I went on: "I considered it a tragedy that you wanted to push yourself to extreme exhaustion. Nobody needs to do that much. What do you consider a crime?" She summarized her position: "Depriving the world of what you have to contribute. It would be tragic if it happens [that] you do not realize your potential out of sheer laziness or cowardice. I could not pardon myself for not having the courage to face a problem and cope with it. Yet I would not face the problem to develop myself completely. Until I give up the low weight, I cannot do anything in the real world. Until now I could not conceive of myself not staying skinny."

Anorexics are masters in disguising or dissociating feelings. With few exceptions they have difficulties in expressing their negative feelings. More likely feelings manifest themselves as failure in gaining weight or as becoming silent in therapy sessions. But patients disguise feelings in different ways. Ida expressed her doubts indirectly. Toward the end of the second year of therapy she became restless and repeatedly asked whether psychiatric treatment was still necessary. She felt that her relationships with other people, particularly her peers, were much better. She still was surprised that people were open and liked her without her having to do anything special. This had been a topic of much discussion, that she never had the feeling of being accepted just for who she was but always felt that she had to earn acceptance at every step.

After reviewing several other difficulties I stated, "Then your question about why you need a psychiatrist seems a little bit premature." Her answer was "Yes, but let's say I feel it has boiled down to something concrete. I feel we are searching too much for what is wrong with me." My reply was strong: "I disagree. Something very important is wrong with you. You do not have a positive opinion of yourself, you do not accept yourself the way you truly are. This self-devaluation and doubt of how can anybody like me, and the terror when you said, 'But 80 pounds—then I'll hate myself'—that was your own reaction. I have not been able to see anything hateful in you, though you have talked a lot about self-hatred." Her response was interesting: "I am afraid that I am going to become over-vain because I have been receiving so many compliments," to which I answered, "That would be perfectly all right. A little bit of vanity is nice."

During the following sessions she repeatedly came back to the theme that things were going very well and that she liked what she was doing. I reminded her, "You *liked* being 66 pounds—you *liked* being hungry." She corrected me, stating that she now felt at ease and no longer pressured: "There is not much that still needs to be worked out. I need the conviction that I won't feel lonely." I added, "And also feel harmony and contentment about your body, and feel comfortable in close relationships." She then admitted that she was still confused about close friendships though she felt at ease in passing friendships. I repeated that I was concerned about her inner self-doubt, the feeling that there was nothing lovable in her, and I added, "How do you feel about your body?" Her answer was "I ignore it." She felt she was not so compulsive anymore, "But I still swim eighty laps a day—and still worry about 'having a stomach.' That is the way I am. I don't like it when other girls are skinny. I accepted only recently that being soft and feminine could be attractive. I always felt it was disgusting. I wondered how anybody found it attractive to be voluptuous."

This doubt about the necessity for continued therapy had an entirely different flavor from her earlier objections, which were that she came only because she did not want to argue with her mother. It gave us an opportunity to reevaluate treatment goals, and a decided change became evident. Instead of exposing difficulties and explaining faulty behavior, our work now could be formulated as a search for undeveloped aspects of her personality, of encouragement to develop qualities that had never matured in her. Ida's tendency to agree with what had been clarified in therapy without truly integrating the new ideas had often resulted in her gradually losing sight of the newly acquired view and returning to the old version. True integration could take place only if the new understanding was explored in the whole emotional context. The fact that Ida actively expressed doubts was important factor in her integrating the new understanding.

I give here a part of our dialogue about the sense of selfhood, taken from the middle of a session. My comment was "What we have been talking about the last few weeks was the failure of your being your own person." She took up the theme: "I wanted to comment on something about that, when I went shopping I felt like I looked like something out of *The Great Gatsby*. I realized while shopping I was asking myself, 'Who do you want to be, what style?' And suddenly it shocked me to realize how much I'm not being my own person but just trying to fill a mold. In this case it was just simply to enjoy taking a role, but I have always had the decision of what role I want to take. And I enjoy it, but I'm always on the stage, so to speak. And the few times that I am myself—well, actually, I am myself more of the time than I realize."

I expressed doubt: "In your behavior here you have been trying to persuade me that to fit somebody else's construct was the highest goal in life. I am very concerned about it, because our goal is for you to accept, or permit to come into the fore, what you truly are, and to live as that. And you consider being disciplined, pursuing other people's goals, as the highest achievement, and you become apologetic whenever you have protested against that."

She took up her position: "Well, right now I'm basically trying to sort out what is me and what is the caricature." I answered, "Fine. But it is my function to help you sort it out. And if you keep these questions quietly to yourself, I cannot help you. In relation to me you have sometimes shown some trust, 'Help me.' But most of the time is spent 'Look here how well I am doing,' and 'Everything is practically fine,' and you know there are still many things that need correcting instead of 'Everything is fine, and I won't change a thing.' As you have heard so often, unless you can express your emotions as they come up—and they may be very rude, they may be very inappropriate, they may be exaggerated, I don't care, but it all must come up. If you try to quietly sort it out on your own and kind of give me little glimpses, things will remain distorted."

Fawn: Less Is More

Fawn's attitude about her eating habits was quite different from those of Ida and Annette; it was partly mystical and partly playful. As noted in the preceding chapter, she had been very much opposed to treatment. She flatly refused to talk about the weight loss or how it had come about, though she made vague references to both her father and me that some people were able to live on air.

When Fawn's intravenous feeding was discontinued she came to my office for her treatment sessions. During one session I drew her attention to the fact that I had remained completely uninformed on many things, including her eating patterns. I mentioned that the internist too had felt that he did not have enough information about her food intake. The doctors' ignorance seemed to please her: "Well, everybody is always going to be unsure how much I eat, because I prefer being vague. You can be jolly sure that if I am sure of what I eat I will either do something bizarre or not eat at all. I like things to be a little vague; they suit me better. I eat more when it's vague. If I can see actually how much it is I won't eat as much or at all. That's the problem with a piece of meat. Well, I'm just a visual person—it still applies, and you can decide whether it's anorexic or whatever you want.

"The truth is, if you give me two portions of peas and mix them up in a great big bowl of rice and let me have as much time as I like and have a nice coffee and sit here with a friend, I may eat all the peas. I may pick each one out and enjoy it. I may have put some mustard on each one if I like, or mayonnaise, or goodness knows what, whatever I happen to see around. If there was some saffron I might use it, or basil, or caraway seeds. But give me half that portion of peas sitting like that on a plate and I probably won't touch a single pea—that's true."

I stated that she seemed to emphasize the playful aspects of eating and the social setting. She agreed: "That's right, and if it's not a game I'm not going to eat. I mean, how do you think I eat a bowl of vegetable soup, bite by bite? Heavens, no. I pick out the corn first, then I pick out the peas, then I think—'Hm, now I'll pick out the alphabet letters.' If I can't play with it, it's no fun. I'm not going to eat something just to eat it." It had been reported that she had spent endless hours in restaurants, and she now gave an explanation. "They can't remove your plate as long as there is food on it." She had illustrated her interests in eating places by the hours she had spent in the cafeteria at the hospital, but she had not talked about it.

Later in that same session she spoke for the first time about her attitude toward her weight: "As far as the weight is concerned, I like being thin. I like feeling thin, I like the 'less' experience more than the 'more' experience. I like the nonconsciousness of the body, and if there was food, I was conscious of it. There were times when I consciously ate great bowls of vegetables and I knew it was only X amount of nutrition or whatever. I wanted to make it as simple as possible. I believe in simple things and I finally got my diet down so simple, with a few extra additions on the side, that I might have felt comfortable in my head—and that matters a lot, whether something is comfortable in my head. But it just couldn't function for my body, because I'm just not going to eat enough peanut butter or cashew butter or whatever it is to stay alive on one thing. That's not the way it works. As it turned out, I got so streamlined that I just about streamlined myself out of existence."

After having spent the whole time denying any similarity to anorexia nervosa she added, quite relaxed, "I suppose every anorexic comes across with a new, different tale about food. There have been so many queer things that I have done about food in my life, and there would still be things that would be difficult for you to come up with. I may be wrong, but I would imagine it would be a little different growing up with all the A's, X's, and Y's about food. Another thing was to figure out how to play with it well enough so that I could extend dinner, because dinner to me was the most wonderful thing around. At dinner you have a chance to communicate with another person, and they were there and wouldn't walk—" Suddenly her mood changed and she added, "Most meals at home were—hell. It was a very extraordinary experience at the dinner table." She became vague in what she said and quite confused and repeated her old formula, "No, because you don't understand. I can just see what you are trying to say. The tenseness did not have to do with what I had to eat. I was never forced to eat."

She was responsive to my comment about her eating so much chili in the hospital cafeteria. "You see, now that's another thing. It's something so spicy that I can't be conscious of it filling me up because I'm conscious of the spice in my mouth. Now that was the wonderful trick with the pepper and the mustard that I could play on myself."

Eventually, although it was not easy for her to eat, she decided to eat sufficient amounts. "It comes more naturally to eat less. It is not too hard for me to see how I might have gotten more skinny as distinct from getting more fat. I was persuaded by various beliefs in nonsalt, nonsugar, and those were very real. Well, I got into trouble without sufficient glucose. I also developed a tremendous craving for salty things. But I did without so many things that I undid my body. Also, it seems to me that I was not so much persuaded by the need for physical, earth-plane nourishment as I now believe myself to be. I mean, there is a definite commitment inside me to good health and sufficient intake of protein. What I am trying to tell you is that it's not the most natural thing in the world for me to eat. Now I have made that commitment, and it makes a very big difference. It still may not be as easy for me as for others, but that is immaterial because I have made the commitment and the belief in the need is there."

When Fawn came to what turned out to be the last session she made some spontaneous statements about her eating. "It is no longer air or thoughts that nourish me. For me to live most well in this incarnation I know I have to accept physical nourishment." She went into some detail about how horrible it was to be physically so weak as she had been and that she was now committed not to permit such a development again. She felt her attitude toward life had changed: "I am making the commitment to involve myself in living."

DISTURBED CONCEPTS OF FOOD, BODY, AND SELF

Helen: The Anxiety of Feeling Well

Some anorexics are reluctant to talk about food at all and treat it as a great secret. Others will talk incessantly or describe patterns that do not sound realistic. Helen, whom we met in chapter 5 and who had vigorously protested against treatment, belonged to this latter group. She was sure that at college, away from home and its supervision, she would gain weight and therefore did not need treatment.

While she came back to see me a month later, her situation sounded quite different. Things were not working out at all. In particular, she was not gaining and was not dating. She was so frightened about this that she asked for help and came into treatment. For the next six weeks she kept her appointments and worked actively. She declared repeatedly that she would not go home for any vacation until she had gained some weight because she could not stand the continuous arguments about her weight. Nevertheless, a week before the Thanksgiving holiday she announced that she was going home for two weeks. "I'll go home and rest and eat, rest and sleep and eat—that's all. That's all I want to do, all I care about. I'm not going to see any friends—I'm too skinny. I don't want to shop for clothes—I'm too skinny. I don't want to do anything—I'm too skinny. I just want to rest and eat." She claimed that was what she had been doing the last few weeks, resting and eating—notwithstanding the fact that she had lost some weight. "I can only tell you how I feel about eating. I am the one who lives in this body. I know when I'm afraid of food and when I'm not. I know that when I first came to see you I was talking about not being able to eat because the food was talking to me and saying 'Fat, fat, fat.' It doesn't do that anymore, and I have been drinking milk and eating butter and fried foods and ice cream and everything I can get my hands on. You should see what I do. Yesterday I ate and ate and ate because I was starving, and I felt good about it. Then I went to my room and ate again. Then I went to bed and said, 'That was good.' And then I woke up at two A.M. and I ate some more."

Despite these assertions, the fact was that she weighed less than when she had come three months earlier. When I mentioned this to her, she said, "I am doing fine. You can panic, but I'm the one who knows when the food talks to me and when it doesn't. It is not talking to me anymore, and I'm going home and I'm looking forward to going home. It bothers me when you get all worried when I'm feeling like I'm coming out on top. What if I hadn't been eating so well? When I have been this busy before I would lose weight. I just don't want you to worry. I believe everything that you have told me and it is starting to take effect in my mind. I just don't particularly like this timing."

Helen reported that she was pleased with the progress she had made in another area: "Can I tell you one good thing that is off the subject? This is making me happy. In some way I feel I've made progress in learning how to get along with people and be less aggressive. Believe it or not—the way I'm shouting at you right now, it doesn't sound like I'm less aggressive—but I think I can slow down a little bit with people and let them talk instead of always being the instigator and asking all the questions. I want to go home with these nice warm feelings toward them, my family."

It looked as if the vacation nearly worked out the way she said. Helen's parents phoned to express their pleasure that Helen was so much more relaxed and capable of being warm, and they were grateful that she had been happier and more self-assertive without being aggressive. But they were terribly alarmed that she had eaten practically nothing and had spent hours on the tennis court. Helen's own report was enthusiastic: "I relaxed, and I ate a whole lot, and I have been doing good ever since I got back, so good that I am nervous about it." "Doing good" meant eating and gaining weight. "I already feel I'm out of it. I'm worried about when I go home and everybody says 'Oh, she has gained weight.' I'm worried if I'm going to be able to handle it. That's what I'm here for, to talk about that. See, I start to eat just a little bit and I think everything is different right away. I take the whole anxiety on at one time, the anxiety of feeling well, as if I weighed 120 pounds right now." Her weight at that time was just about 80 pounds.

She went into detail about how much improvement she expected if she would only eat a meal. I made a cautionary comment at this time: "Eating and gaining weight are not magic that makes good things happen." Her reply was angry: "Well, it's supposed to be. That's what everybody has been promising me." I corrected her, stating that at no time had I promised this. "All I can promise is that you will be less tense and self-centered and anxious, and that in order to have close relationships you have to put an honest effort into it." She protested, "I take charge and I'm eating food, and then I feel alone and I feel scared because I'm letting go of my sickness and I'm left with nothing. I'm left with no boyfriend and nothing to hide behind. I feel like I've let go of my cover and there I am with nothing to hide me from the world, anxiety, and anything."

She interrupted treatment at that time but stayed in touch with the internist who, after a few months, referred her back to me because she was depressed and her weight was below 80 pounds. I insisted that she had to take treatment seriously and not as an on-and-off affair. For the following few months she was deeply interested in the therapeutic work and began to come to a better understanding of her problems.

During the next Thanksgiving weekend she was in a store and saw herself in a three-way mirror, and she was shocked to see how bony her upper arm was: "like an animal, not like a human being. It looks so weird from the back, how it is all flat here and then it goes in and gets real tiny. It looks like all there is, is bone. I just was stunned." She admitted that she hadn't gained anything. "My present weight is 83—but let me finish talking before you say anything more to turn me off. In the past I have actually gone by my feeling—this was another lie that I believed in. If I ate and was full, then somehow I actually would think that my body had changed that quickly. I promise, that's what I used to think and do. I would eat and then I would feel full, and I would think 'That's the end—I'm full, so I must be better. So that's all I need to do.'"

At one point in a therapy session, she announced defiantly, "I'm not going to eat dinner, because I'm not hungry anymore. See, that happens when I do whatever they talk me into doing. There is no way I'm going to be hungry in two hours. I would go out at nine o'clock when I get hungry." She explained how she wanted dinner to be perfect: "I want every meal to be perfect. I want my friends to be there, I want the food to be good, and I want all the boys to be there. I want it to be pleasurable." I responded to her sarcastic tone, "You are telling me, 'You see, you can't make me eat.' I can only repeat I can't make you eat and don't intend to. It is up to you."

In an entirely different context Helen described her attitude toward food and weight as "I'm so scared to put any weight on. I don't want my pants to fit any tighter. I think if anybody ever looked at me and said, 'Gee, you are putting on weight.

146

I can see a little rear; you are getting a little fanny,' I would jump out of the window and commit suicide. If anybody ever said, 'Gee, Helen, you look fatter. Your face looks better. You are putting on a little weight,' you might as well kill me. You might as well take out a gun and shoot me. I am so afraid of those words."

Megan: A "Perfect" Size 1

In contrast to Helen's sporadic and impulsive decisions about eating, Megan was highly organized and could practically predict her weight for every day. The father of this twenty-two-year-old college student phoned for an appointment for his oldest daughter because she had adjustment problems and was excessively thin. She was a good student and was quite slim, with 110 pounds having been her highest weight. She had gone to an out-of-town college but was completely unprepared to live away from home, and had became depressed and had to leave. She was hospitalized for a while, mainly for pharmacological treatment, but she also had "deep analysis," talks with her psychiatrist. After she recovered from the depression she decided she did not like the way she looked and lost weight, down to 80 pounds. After a year her parents began talking about hospitalization again to help her regain the weight.

At the time of the consultation Megan had regained some weight and was just below the 100-pound mark. She talked quite freely about her weight history. To my question "How do you see this weight problem?" she answered, "I don't see it as a problem at all, not at all. In the past I think the lowest

I got was about 80 pounds. I had wanted to lose weight; I was dissatisfied with the way I looked, so I decided to lose weight, and so I did." At this point I commented that it was usually not quite so simple, that most people talk about dieting and will lose a few pounds, but then they stop. Her response was "But not when they are very determined. And I am very much so. As I told you already, I'm a perfectionist. When I set out to do something, when I put my mind to it, I do it. When I determined I was going to lose weight, there was never any problem. I know I lost a lot—I liked it. But it seemed to me that nobody else did. Everybody was saying 'Oh, you are too thin, you are too skinny.' But I must say that some of my best times were when I was small. I also felt that I had a lot more energy, if you can believe that. I ate good things, but very small amounts. I think this energy was all nervous; I know I could never do it again."

She described the exact amounts she ate at three meals, with nothing in between, no snacks. She had felt quite pleased with the result of her restricted intake. After she felt forced to gain weight—and she felt that she had been forced—her stomach could not take dieting anymore. "It growls. It's stretched." She was very vague in describing her eating, except to say that she started to have snacks between meals. She stuck very much to the same kinds of things she had eaten while losing weight, leaving out mainly starches, bread, and sweets. She felt she was on a good diet now and that whether she gained or not was entirely in her hands: "I have programmed my mind, there are things that I do not want to eat ever again, ever. For instance, bread. I have restricted myself to only 'good' things, like vegetables and fruit. And I didn't eat, and I still don't eat, bread or cake or cookies or chocolate. I just was not eating these things. And I think that has helped my allergies, and I feel fine as far as nutrition goes."

She continued, "Now that I have gained some weight, why is it that now I feel like I'm getting lazy? I don't have that old discipline. Before, I feel like I had control of everything, and I liked that feeling. I like to know that if I wanted to gain weight I could do it, and if I don't want to, I don't. But now I feel like I'm out of control. It's really funny, because when I weighed a lot less than I do now I had so much energy. I mean, I could do fifty projects at once and I didn't have to work so hard at my grades. I don't have that energy and the drive that I had when I was thin. That's really scary for me to cope with. I don't like it at all. I feel like I kind of lost some control and some energy—and I don't have the discipline that I once had."

I asked her how she had felt when she looked so slim. "Did you look terrible to yourself at that time?" She described, "No, I didn't. I didn't really notice it very much, because I've always been thin. The thing that I liked more than anything was the fact that I felt like I had control of what I ate and what I did, and that nobody was telling me what to do. And I liked the fact that—I hate to say this, and it is hard for me to say it, but I know it to be true—it got me recognition. Because one of the main things that I hated and still do—even now it is very difficult for me to go into a store and have to say 'Yes, I want a size 5,' because to me that seems so common. Before I could go in and say 'I want a size 1,' and everybody would just look around. It was like the whole store, everybody standing around, would go, 'Golly, you are thin—that must be nice.' And everybody, 'Oh, that's great—you can find all these clothes, and everything is made for slender people nowadays, and how wonderful it must be to be thin.' It seemed to me that before that I was real common; all my friends seem to wear size 5 or 7, and I didn't like just being one of the crowd."

In discussing her regaining weight, she added, "I don't want it to go up to 100—not right now. I do that because I'm having all these feelings about losing control. I do it in five-pound intervals. I say, 'Boy, if I can get it to 95 and see how I feel'—when I say 'feel' I'm talking about mentally—and see how I really feel about it. If it feels okay, if I feel like I'm not losing control, that I still have the reins, then I'll go up and push it to 100." I asked, "But why are you so afraid of losing control?" She answered, "Because really that's the only thing I have control over. And because I feel like if I lose that, I lose everything. I just don't want to lose control of that. I want to be always thought of as thin."

Nora: The Competitor

Nora developed ritualistic ways of eating quite early and became obsessive in her thinking about food and weight. She had been ill with anorexia less than a year when she came for consultation, and her weight was low but not life-threatening. She was a good observer and would describe in detail how situations had developed. "Lately I have not been hungry—but I make myself eat." When asked whether she still remembered when she had enjoyed food, she gave an evasive answer: "At that time I did not pay attention to it." She felt that she still liked food but no longer had hunger or desire for it. "Now I'm not very hungry, but all I think about is food. Afterward I often feel it would have been good to eat."

Nora had not known about anorexia nervosa until the previous summer when she went on a trip with a group of girls, and one of the girls developed the illness. When Nora decided to lose some weight, she was cautious because she did not know what she was going to look like after losing weight. She soon lost more than she had planned and then became preoccupied with maintaining the low weight. She decidedly did not want to regain anything, and then she wanted to lose more. "I also decided that if everything else went wrong I could always be skinny." She felt that keeping her weight low would give her reassurance against having "nothing." It also was reassuring to be low in weight when she went to an out-of-town college.

Some anorexics consider their eating behavior their deepest secret; others experience it entirely in competitive terms. Nora, when she was home for a vacation weekend, mentioned, "I think of all the people I am competing with at school, the ones who don't eat, and then I bet they are not eating over Thanksgiving. It applies even to snacks or ice cream. One of my friends from high school lost weight when she went to college, and when I want to eat ice cream, I think, 'I bet she doesn't do it,' and then I can't eat it either."

Nora reported about her progress at Thanksgiving time: "It seems so crazy for me to think about food when I am not hungry. That's when I'm afraid I'm going to go out of control, when I still think about food when I am not hungry. It is so weird to eat something heavy and still think about food when I know I am not hungry and my stomach is full. How am I ever going to know when I've had enough?"

Remarks like this become the leitmotif of her concern. The illness was much more drawn out than I had originally expected, and Nora repeated this concern about thinking about food when not hungry over and over again. She developed the habit of having a cookie late at night regardless of how she felt or what she had eaten. "When I eat something fattening it is easier to eat at night. So I look forward to eating a cookie, my one cookie, late at night—I eat it really slow, and I have to eat it by myself. I wait until the night after I have eaten a big dinner. I am not hungry for the cookie, I'm still thinking about it: 'Oh, that is the time when I get to eat my cookie, even if I'm not hungry for it.' "

As time went on she became more and more worried about this habit: "I get my only happiness from eating that cookie. Then I think I'm going to start eating to be happy. That gives me the fear that I will be unhappy about everything, and be happy about eating a cookie. Then it makes me afraid that I'm going to cure all my unhappiness by eating and eating cookies all the time, because my greatest fear is to lose control and to become fat."

I explained to her that she sounded as if she were afraid of never having other sources of satisfaction. She agreed: "It is still hard to have a close relationship with someone, because I'm still not on firm ground. I'm still not sure of my responses."

CHAPTER 7

Childhood Revisited

Eﬞ VER SINCE anorexia nervosa was first described in the literature, the question of the family's role in its development and in treatment has been widely debated. Some professionals rate the family's importance as little or nonexistent, whereas others see the interaction in the family as the key to all issues and treatment problems. One of the puzzles about anorexia nervosa is its sudden occurrence in seemingly normal, or even superior, children who have grown up in privileged, stable homes. When anorexia nervosa was still rather rare, the demographic descriptions of the families were amazingly similar. Specifically, the families were of high social status and great wealth, with few broken marriages; and the parents, more often the father, were middle-aged when the child was born. The fathers were often in their sixties or seventies when the illness became manifest. Psychological characteristics included a great restraint in emotional expression within the family, little contact between the patient and the father (except in unusual circumstances), and excessive closeness to the mother. These features were considered more or less preconditions for anorexia nervosa. More recently, with higher incidence of the illness, the family background is no longer so exclusively that of great wealth or social prominence. However, the aspiration level is high in comparison to the achievements of other families in the social group to which these particular families belong. The fathers are unusually successful, self-made men, and moving into upper-class society presents something of a problem for these families. In one family the college-age children refused to visit their parents' new home in an upper-class neighborhood. In another highly successful family it was the mother who refused to participate in the life style of upper-class society. But whether the family's wealth is old or new, the anorexic child feels unable to live up to what she considers the parents' high expectations.

With few exceptions, parents will describe their home as happy and the anorexic child as having been unusually good, cooperative, and satisfying. Patients may at first agree that there had been no difficulties and will praise the superior features of their home and family. However, it is important to clarify what was going on during the patient's early life, because misleading attitudes if unchallenged, can be carried through life. As treatment progresses and the patient begins to relax her rigid attitude toward her past and begins to trust her own thinking, the picture of perfection gradually changes. This reevaluation of the circumstances of her childhood represents an important aspect of the anorexic's treatment.

It is often quite difficult to get facts about the patient's early life, because the parents have transformed their recollection into consistent praise for her ideal childhood behavior. The picture must be slowly pieced together from a developmental point of view, with the knowledge that the picture will change a good deal as treatment progresses. There are few conditions with such great discrepancies as there are between the childhood events as told by the parents and the inner experiences of the child who has lived through them. This universal discrepancy illustrates the seriousness of the problem. The way in which the child (now probably grown up) has experienced and remembered what went on during childhood is markedly different from what the parents remember. And this misinterpretation continues into adult experiences. Working toward clarification so that patient and parents can communicate is an important aspect of treatment.

Problems in communication are one factor that make the dynamic pattern of childhood experiences in anorexics difficult to recognize. Experiences that are reconstructed on the basis of what is communicated in treatment may be quite contradictory. This is not a deliberate distortion of the facts but the result of discrepancies in the perception of events in childhood. It is quite difficult for most anorexics to present the facts as they have taken place, because their upbringing did not foster clear and independent observation and thinking. They have been taught to be "good" and to behave well, but they have few spontaneous feelings or experiences. In families like theirs, people are nice to each other but never express any other feelings. Contact with the parents reveals what the family atmosphere has been. The politeness may be so excessive that it is difficult to get factual information.

What is going on in these families to produce a child who

is unable to face life? This is not an easy question to answer because the factors may be rather subtle. More often than not the family offers, at least on the surface, a picture of devoted child care, of exposure to educational and cultural opportunities, of doing "the right thing" in many ways. The exaggerated goodness may be an expression of underlying difficulties.

The difficulties in these families will be found in the patterns of interaction that result in the child's being handicapped in her own sense of autonomy. In these families that appear to be well functioning, I often encounter disregard for the child's expressed or implied wishes. Frequently the mothers determine the child's activities, plan everything ahead of time, and try to raise the child in their own image. The children in turn fail to develop the feeling of having a personality of their own, but experience having lived their life through another person. Such mothers claim that they have complete understanding of everything the child wants and assign their own feelings to the child. In a way, these patients have never faced living situations in which their own feelings and wants are recognized and validated. An important part of the treatment process is clarifying and correcting the conclusions that were derived from these distorting early experiences, whether or not they were justified and in agreement with the factual events and actual experiences.

Early in treatment many of these patients will talk about the superior features of their home and family, expressing guilt for having disturbed that picture. It takes considerable time for the patient to develop trust in herself and in the therapist and begin to open up and tell "the true story," the way she had experienced life and the people and events that characterized her childhood. The slowness of this process is in itself an illustration of the deficits in the patients' communication, especially in identifying and expressing feelings. Even after the idea of family perfection has been confronted in therapy and the patient is able to repeat the therapist's reconstruction of less-than-perfect events, her more spontaneous feeling that things had been perfect will remain for quite a while. A reevaluation of this "perfection" reveals the extent to which the patient had lived her life through someone else.

Though clarifying early experiences and relationships and reinterpreting them in realistic terms are central tasks of therapy, many—if not most—anorexics are reluctant to reexamine the features of their background that helped to coerce them into the anorexic corner. Occasionally the recognition or admission of difficulties comes like a sudden revelation during a consultation. Yet many resist this exploration, and after months, even years, in treatment, they still cling to their old concept of the perfect home.

Annette: Alone on an Island

Annette's early years illustrate many features common to the development of anorexia. The childhood picture that evolved was one of great loneliness and isolation, with little chance to check or countercheck her experiences with her parents or siblings. She expressed her extreme isolation as feeling like the lady in the harbor (the Statue of Liberty), "like the statue, untouched and untouchable, on a little island in the gray ocean, with no relationship to anybody or anything." She spoke with open regret about the many wasted years in which she had kept away from the human contact.

Annette's relationship with her parents was dominated by

the conviction that she had to avoid ever deserving blame or criticism. She would never do anything that might arouse their disapproval. The great strain of her childhood was to figure out what "they" wanted her to do, what "they" would encourage or would honestly permit her. She was aware that they wanted her to be kind and considerate, but beyond that she felt she was under continuous strain to outguess them, to find out what they truly wanted. She used double-track thinking so as never to confront them with the dilemma of asking permission for something of which she was not sure that they would honestly approve.

She remembered one episode from dancing class when she was about twelve or thirteen years old. One boy started to pay attention to her. She liked him too, and at first she was pleased when he asked her to go to a movie with him. However, she did not have the courage to ask her parents' permission; she did not know how they would respond but was convinced that they would react unfavorably to her asking them at all. She went through several days of doubting, became increasingly miserable and unhappy, and could not sleep, worrying whether to ask her parents or to let the boy down. When he came to her house on the appointed day she sent him away with the explanation that she had developed a cold and could not go. The torture of this dilemma had been so harassing that she made sure it would never occur again. She made it a maxim of her life never again to arouse a boy's interest. Thus she isolated herself in one more area from all social and possibly sexual experiences.

She was puzzled by one of her older sisters, because she seemed to have a relaxed and warm relationship with her parents despite having what Annette considered a negative-sounding experience with them. While this sister was at boarding school, a sailing trip was planned for which the students needed their parents' permission. The parents said no and the sister obeyed, but she *knew* that they were wrong, that it would have been a good experience for her and she should have gone. The sister felt this had been a turning point in her relationship to the parents. She had a clear-cut concept of her having been right and decided that from then on she needed to rely on her own judgment. Her sense of independence stands in marked contrast to Annette's attitude, which was one of eternal self-torture, as she was convinced that her parents would disapprove of whatever she wanted. To Annette the greatest danger was that they might not say openly how they felt and would then leave her with the ordeal of trying to figure out how to avoid their unexpressed wrath.

Increasingly in therapy the topic of inquiry turned to the significance, meaning, and potentially distorting effect of seemingly positive experiences. The ways in which outwardly excellent child care could result in serious deficits in the child's grasp of reality gradually became clearer.

A specific example comes from a childhood memory that sounded pleasant enough. At cocktail parties Annette had taken the role of "mother's helper": she would pass nuts and celery sticks around. She did not like this task, but her mother convinced her, saying, "They want to see you." Annette noted that the guests were fleetingly interested in her but then turned back to their own conversations. "All these ritualistic things, they never seemed true. The things they said and the way they acted were because of my parents, not on account of me," she stated.

I agreed with her and enlarged: "That is one of the tragedies of your life, that in this well-meaning home into which you were born, you experienced 'I am only an appendix; they don't give me genuine recognition.' The question now is whether you want to go through life clinging to this unhappy childhood image, or whether you will be able to reexamine and revisit it. I realize that is how it looked to you then, but I can also see that it doesn't represent the complete or true reality. You never believed that people acknowledged you for your genuine self, even if they did." Her response was pessimistic: "People always have an ulterior motive. The reason they were nice to me then was to please my parents, and now it is for feeling sorry for me."

I persisted with my reasoning: "The real question is whether you are able and willing to believe that you are a worthwhile person the way you are, not only if you are transformed into something superperfect. You have denied feeling worthwhile to yourself all your life, not deliberately, but because you believed that these unhappy childhood experiences were the whole story. When Mother said 'They all want to see you' you doubted it the way you doubted when she told you 'Oh, you were a big hit.' You didn't know whether she really meant it or just said it to make you feel good—and now you still don't know yourself whether you have done well." Annette repeated the often-made statement that she had always thought they were giving her too much. I replied that the problem was that "you felt you didn't deserve as much as they gave you. Either way, the problem is that you underrate yourself. The dilemma is how a child in your particular family can get a true measure of what the child contributes. *They* all are so big and do big things—successful and admirable things. Sister played the piano better, Mother painted better, Father did these important jobs out in the big world. Whatever it was, they all did big things. How can a child get a measure of her own importance, or the hope that she will measure up?"

An outstanding feature of Annette's childhood was that she never daydreamed about herself as a grown-up, a person with a future and a life of her own. Though her sisters had big weddings when she was six or seven years old, she never thought about her own wedding or about having children. She did not play with dolls, considering it a "waste of time." Even in her twenties she continued to feel like the child in her parents' home. She felt her lot in life was to stay with her parents. Annette had known families in which a maiden daughter took care of aged parents. In her own fantasies her parents had become senile, invalid, or mentally incompetent so that they needed her. In this way she could finally show her devotion and love.

The strength of this concept that she would be forever part of her parents' home came vividly into the open when her father, in one of his letters, mentioned quite casually that they were considering selling the house. Annette had a severe emotional reaction to the idea that her parents would even consider selling their home: "They must not do it. . . . The house is me—that's where I grew up, and nobody would know about the way we lived or that I had a home if they sell it." She felt the home represented not only her own identity but also her desire to give love and appreciation to her parents. Because the family had never talked about feelings, "saving the house" was expressive of what she did not express in words. In connection with this strong reaction, I learned much not only about the emotionally inhibited way in which the family interacted, but also about Annette's feelings that she was always "in the way" or "something extra" for whom there was no real place.

Though somewhat shy throughout her childhood, Annette always had friends, with varying degrees of closeness. Before school she had played with little boys in the neighborhood, and her discovery about sex differences left her with a feeling of the unfairness of Nature. When she entered school she became even more convinced of the unfairness, but now it was in relation to other girls. The girls who were tough and athletic were accepted in the boys' group, and those were the girls she envied and with whom she wanted to compete. The other girls, the dollhouse girls, were nice the way she was, but she did not feel she belonged to that group either.

For Annette this was the beginning of the conviction that she never belonged wholeheartedly anywhere, that she was forever condemned to be on the fringe. Her best friend, who was very active and aggressive, was convinced that whatever she did was the thing to do, and felt that she herself was the center. Annette went along with her activities but never shared her positive conviction about herself.

Things became even more difficult in seventh or eighth grade, when the girls who in the lower grades had been leaders in athletics, and who had been rather contemptuous of the "sissy" girls, now became aggressive in establishing boy-girl rapport. Annette began to feel even more on the fringe. She did not know with whom to make friends, because to be in the social group you had to be skillful and active in handling boys, and she simply did not know how to behave, what to talk about, whether to kiss or not, and what sex was about. Her solution to this dilemma was to make herself "more perfect," and this decision seems to be related to her increasing concern about her body.

She had noticed that men could eat as much as they wanted, whereas girls were dainty and concerned about gaining weight. She had grown in height rather quickly and was quite slender. In fact, her pediatrician was concerned about her gaining sufficient weight relative to her fast growth. While the other girls considered her lucky to be so slim, Annette tried to be feminine by eating like the other girls. In her effort to show that she was like a girl she was careful in what she ate and would refuse dessert, just as the others did.

The dissatisfaction about her social position carried over into the academic field. Though she was an excellent student, she was never satisfied. To give just one example: Annette was good at writing short stories and received high grades and praise from her teacher. She felt that she was lucky in having a teacher who liked the way she wrote. However, at the time she began the anorexic regime Annette believed her imagination left her, though she continued to get good grades for her writing. That to her was proof that the teacher felt sorry for her, and she felt embarrassed about receiving such good grades.

Two points of Annette's internal confusion were illustrated by her dissatisfaction with her school performance. One was that she never was sure for whom she achieved; it certainly was not for herself but mainly to please her father. However, her image of what he wanted her to achieve or expected her to do was rather vague and quite unrealistic. The other confusing aspect was that achieving was really proving that she was like a man; her accomplishments were not expressions of her own interests or enjoyment but things that would look to the outside world as if they had been done by a man. It gradually became clear that whatever she achieved was unsatisfactory; the achievement neither turned her into a male nor reassured her that Father's wishes had been fulfilled.

She felt that her need to restrain herself, "to carry on through thick and thin," was related to the fact that she was overindulged as a child. She compared her upbringing with what she had learned about her older siblings: "It wasn't quite fair. They grew up during the war years and things were rationed. They also lived in a smaller house. I always felt their way was the right way. I was being treated too soft and too indulged." She vividly remembered her sisters' often-made comment: "Isn't she spoiled?" Though these words were apparently used jokingly and with affection, Annette concluded that being spoiled was a shameful attribute for a child, and she devoted her life to appearing "not spoiled." In order to appear "not spoiled," she never expressed a wish for anything, material or otherwise, and she accepted gifts and privileges only because she could not stop them. Yet she never felt justified to receive them. Her well-to-do parents were deeply devoted to her. Thus she received many gifts, each one evoking the obligation to prove that she was worthy of it. A few gifts were satisfying and reassuring, ones she felt were truly meant for her, not something her parents felt obliged to give her. Her father's work involved foreign travel, and Annette remembered warmly that he brought back foreign dolls in his briefcase. These she accepted with love and gratitude; they were proof that Father had thought of her while abroad. Most other gifts meant nothing. They just showed her parents' goodness and their doing "the right thing." Annette felt that the gifts made them feel that they were generous and cared for her.

I attempted to help her see how her deductions influenced not only her own thinking and behavior but also that of her parents: "In reality, you must have made it difficult for your parents if you never expressed a wish. In a way you forced them to guess and to give something of their own choosing." Her answer was "But I was already a spoiled child on account of what my parents did. I had the responsibility of doing everything to make myself unspoiled."

She tried to change the topic to the problem of having been deprived of the companionship of young parents but ended up again expressing isolation fear: "I have a niece who is now twelve, and I feel she has a much better relationship to her parents, who are still young." She felt that her older sisters had much more of a family life, "because my parents were young then. All of that being part of a young family, I never had. I was spoiled because *things* were given to me, but not because I did things together with them . . . it goes all the way back. They are not separate people but belong together as a family— they tell each other what they really feel. . . . I still want to be part of their lives. I am frightened by the idea of getting well—I never had plans for being grown up. I cannot conceive of having a home or a family of my own."

I tried to support this painful revelation: "I am glad that your true feelings are coming into the open. You have spent so much time maintaining that your family was perfect and you never talked about what had hurt you, out of fear that it might sound as if you were 'blaming' them. There is nobody to blame. You cannot go through life dominated by the feelings of a lonely and bitter six-year-old child, whose greatest goal was not to make demands, not to become her own person."

She repeated, "I am frightened by the idea of getting well. I still want to be part of their lives. I am no longer part of them, but not of anything else either. I cannot help but feel that I was a mistake. I shall never have the feelings of being part of them. . . . I felt I had to be super nice to deserve the things they gave me, and they lavished them on me, no matter what I did." The lavish gifts, however, did not appease the pain of "not belonging," and this remained a theme in our conversations for quite a long time.

Annette was equally cautious and restrained in describing and evaluating her relationship to her sisters. Annette's early memories about her older sisters were vague. There were two older ones whom she came to know only when they were adults and no longer living at home. Though she was very concerned about their good opinion, to her they were strange grown-up women who visited the home and acted as if they belonged. Josie, the sister who was eight years older than Annette, was a problem, she admitted, but "she meant well." Josie played a negative role in Annette's life not by being aggressive or punitive toward her little sister but by virtually ignoring her, treating her as nonexistent. Annette revealed only gradually how often Josie had been a source of pain and sorrow to her, not so much by what she did but by the way she disregarded Annette. They shared a room when Annette was little, and Annette felt that not calling out when she woke in her crib had to do with her fear of this sister. For one year they went together on the school bus, but Annette had strict orders never to talk to Josie. A sad reflection of her feeling that "the good things in life are not for me" was her attitude toward the candy store. Josie was a teenager at the time and made Annette walk home alone while she stayed with her friends and had a refreshment at the corner candy store. Annette was sad because she had been sent off home, but even more because she was convinced that when her time came and she was a big girl, she would not enjoy going to the candy store. In a way this was a self-fulfilling prophecy, because when she reached that age she was involved in rigid dieting and anorexic behavior.

Annette's need to present a favorable image of her home life was so strong that even after we had covered considerable ground, she was often reluctant to speak openly about her experiences as a child. She took care to have only positive memories about her parents. She would label anything else as "blaming" them—and that would reinforce her negative feelings about herself. As is the case with many anorexic patients, Annette and I had to go over the same incidents repeatedly before she dared to believe in the reliability of her own memories and trust me enough to permit less favorable incidents to come to the surface.

In the early phases of treatment, Annette had been cooperative but was extremely reluctant to clarify the roles of various family members. As discussed in chapter 3, this reluctance persisted until she described how she had experienced the relationship to her sister Josie. The recognition that there were errors in this relationship gave Annette a new sense of freedom, and with this liberation she was ready to discuss and explore her concept of her position in the family and how she had felt excluded from joining the mainstream of life. She attributed the power to exclude her to a sister whom she had always experienced as intimidating and forbidding. After the error of this conviction had been clarified, Annette proceeded to look at her own role in this isolation; how she had, of her own volition, withdrawn from life as if she were a nonperson. The recognition that she could have been so wrong in relation to one person made it possible for her to look at other relationships in a new way. This working through involved a reexamination of many different experiences and relationships.

This change from her seeing herself as a passive victim to acknowledging herself as an active participant in her whole development, in particular in the development of the anorexic illness, was an important turning point in Annette's treatment. In many if not most patients, the anorexic symptom is presented initially as something that has just happened, like a sinister fate that befalls the patient and family. For a true resolution of the underlying problems the patient needs to become aware of her own role in this development. However, coming to a new understanding of one's problems is not enough. For effective change to occur in actual living each point needs to be clarified in its many ramifications.

As mentioned, in the beginning of treatment Annette had spoken in positive and admiring terms about her home and family. It was exceedingly painful for her to acknowledge that there had been experiences within her home that had interfered with her developing a positive self-concept, a sense of her personal worth and value. The early experiences had also left her with a profound basic mistrust about the people around her, and even more about her own worth. She struggled against the conviction that it is the child's fault to have arrived "as an after-thought," always in danger of being made to feel an unwanted nuisance who was in the way. She gradually become more convinced of her right to live her own life and to acknowledge her own feelings and desires. However, Annette also recognized that she was excessively preoccupied with what she called her "image in the eyes of the beholder," and was still skeptical about whether she would ever be able to trust her own genuineness.

I summarized what she had said earlier: "If I understand what you are telling me, you feel your whole life has been a façade performance, where you would show only sweet, compliant, submissive behavior. Isn't that what you called 'the great put-on'?" She admitted that she was afraid to show what was below the surface and added, "I have to hold a tight lid on it." She explained, "When I cried, I was afraid they would be annoyed. Of course they wouldn't ever show it." I commented, "But a child has the right to feel accepted unconditionally, the way she is. You felt that if you showed your real self they would not love you." Annette repeated, "They would never show it if they were irritated, but I would feel that they were."

Here I elaborated: "That is even sadder than what I had assumed thus far. The child is forced continually to guess whether her family is annoyed or not. 'If I am a nuisance they won't love me any more.' But no one showed true feelings to this little girl. This type of interaction is worse for the child, who feels always in danger of being declared a nuisance. Parents who are open with their children may even yell at them if they are angry, but the issue gets settled. In your family nothing was ever out in the open." She agreed: "That's correct. With Father I never knew what he felt. You could not guess what he felt from his face or the way he talked. He never showed his feelings. When I exposed myself, I felt like I was hanging in midair."

I enlarged on every child's need for continuous feedback. She added here, "I got all the positive feedback," to which I responded with an expression of doubt: "But that is only half of it. The question is whether it is genuine or not." Annette then explained how she would second-guess her parents and anticipate which behavior would have their honest approval, so that their reaction would at least appear genuine. She applied it to the story about her nap. "I always knew what they would say if I cried—'Don't be a crybaby.' That's what would have been said. Nothing tough was ever said directly, and I made sure that they would never have a reason to say it." This second-guessing was Annette's way to avoid provoking her parents' disapproval, but it was also an attempt to make their responses literally honest. "I made sure they would say what they really meant, not what they were supposed to say. They could say 'She is such a nice girl,' and it was not only polite and nice, they really meant it." My comment was "But that is assuming that what they show is only their façade." She responded, "They meant most of it. I wanted to behave so that I knew what they said was what they truly meant."

I commented, "Open criticism would have been better than this continual worry about what they really meant. There is something called lack of basic trust. You could believe what they said, but you could never trust what they truly meant." She was convinced that "they would never have expressed negative feelings—though Josie did." Here I made a generalization: "It is a dreadful condition to grow up with the conviction that nobody says what they really think. You gained very early the conviction that pleasing people was more important than clear and honest communication." She felt that this second-guessing was affecting her current relationships with people, such as her coworkers and her roommate. "And I have to be as close to perfect as one can be all the time, to make sure that they are not annoyed or that I would not make them angry." I said something about how much uncertainty this desire to be perfect must create. Annette agreed, "I know I am not easy to communicate with. And I'm not perfect." This I confirmed: "Thank goodness. Who could live with anyone who wants to be perfect? Human frailty leads to conflict. And that is one thing you were deprived of: you have never experienced that conflict is followed by reconciliation. For you the concept of conflict is deadly. Your problem is not feeling disagreement and anger; your problem is that you never dare to express these feelings. You reacted to this, with what you used to call 'the great put-on,' by becoming sick."

Ida: "I Did Not Have the Right to Eat"

Early on, the therapist needs to take an active part in the evaluation of the family background, of the encouraging or difficult aspects of the patient's early life. In Ida's case we used the competition—and the expectation of outstanding performance, which is what she probably heard and understood as more demanding than it really was—to begin the reevaluation of what had happened in her early life.

Ida was cared for by European governesses, all of whom she claimed to have liked. She was always well behaved, and her governesses never had cause to complain about her to her mother. She added, "I knew they all loved me—I made sure they would." I pointed out to her the basic uncertainty that this sentence expressed: that she was sure of their love only as long as she was obedient and compliant. This was one of the first openings we had to recognize some features in her background that had not been superperfect.

Many other opportunities arose for her to recognize experiences that indicated interference with the development of self-reliance, spontaneity, and initiative. There were many strict rules in her home, such as no eating between meals. She clung to this no-snack rule while in college. She would skip meals but would not permit herself to eat anything, however hungry she was, until the next mealtime. As a child she had to eat what was put on her plate, though she had no say in choosing what and how much food was served. Having been forced to eat beyond the point of satiation was one of her few unpleasant memories.

Ida ultimately did well during her first year of treatment, and at the end of her freshman year she was in much better health, less ritualistic and less artificial in her behavior. She went home for a few weeks, but during the first few days she became distressed because she felt she did not belong, she had nothing to contribute, and she was not brilliant enough. An image came to her, that she was like a sparrow in a golden cage, too plain and simple for the luxuries of her home but deprived of the freedom of doing what she truly wanted to do. Cages are made for big, colorful birds who show off their plumage and are satisfied just to hop around. She felt quite different, like a sparrow, inconspicuous and energetic, who wants to fly around and take off on its own, who is not made for a cage. For the first time she spoke openly about the pain and frustration of her childhood as the youngest child in a wealthy home with many rules and regulations. She felt that her own needs and desires had been disregarded and that too many demands were made on her.

She spent the rest of the summer vacation traveling in Europe with a group from her college. When she came back she looked well and had gained some weight. She thought her weight might be approaching 100 pounds but was not sure. She said she looked and felt like she had when she was sixteen and had gone to France. As a matter of fact, she wore a rather chic skirt; the last time she had been able to wear it had been on the previous trip. She had had to discard several garments because they were too small for her now. There was no expressed dislike for her weight at this time, only concern at times that she might gain too much. Though she spoke repeatedly about her fear of not being able to stop eating, she was quite definite that she would not react by cutting down on eating, that she was too much aware of feeling better at a higher weight.

She was somewhat alarmed that she would become depressed easily, which she felt was "absurd," because things had been going her way. She had been well received by her family, she was included in discussions on business affairs where she had formerly felt she was disregarded, and she had a feeling that the others were talking with her on the same level, as a fellow adult. She found herself the family expert on art, and in a peculiar way this shocked her. She had contempt for

anyone who knew less than she did, and that applied to anything. She felt her mother did not want to learn all the details
she now knew: "The very fact that they didn't feel the same
way as I do about things makes me feel isolated." She referred
again to the enjoyable discussions she had had with her father
before his death, about political ideas and philosophical writing. She was concerned that "outside a stimulating environment" she would stop being interested and would then be
unable to contribute to such activities. She also realized that
there had really been no time for long discussions because
family members were so busy with their daily activities at their
vacation spot.

I felt that her progress had been good. Ida was willing to
review her early experiences not in terms of their perfection
but in terms of their contribution to her development, particularly to the difficulties in her early years. About two weeks after
her return from the long summer vacation I mentioned that
we had freely discussed some of her problems in relation to her
mother and brother and various friends, but that she had been
rather secretive about her relationship to her father. I summarized what I felt we had learned thus far, that she had talked
about a special closeness between him and her, and that she
had shared his interest in philosophy and religion. This continued to represent a secret bond between them. From the few
facts she had given, though, I had gained the impression that
in reality she had had little contact with her father and that
she had lived in hope that he would pay more attention to her
as she grew older. She had said repeatedly that if her father had
lived she would not have needed to become sick, that he had
died at the wrong time, that his death had deprived her of
being recognized by him. Her striving for specialness through
excessive discipline and thinness had been her imagined way

of pleasing him and arousing his attention, but it was also an act of defiance.

She listened intensely to my summary and began to cry without reacting verbally to what had been said. In her next session she reported that her anorexic symptoms had come back in full force. She was unable to eat, had increased her laxative consumption, and swam twice as much as before. Within two weeks her weight dropped to 86 pounds and she looked visibly thinner. It was to take nearly four months for her weight to reach 90 pounds again, and nearly a year and a half before it would exceed 95, with many ups and downs. For a while she expressed severe self-accusation when she had gained, for having "given in." This episode resolved whatever doubts she still clung to about the relationship between anorexia and psychological experiences. Ida acknowledged that the weight fluctuations went hand in hand with her emotional and psychological attitude and reactions.

Gradually—very gradually—she spoke about her secret inner life. She believed in life after death and had never accepted the finality of her father's death, but was convinced that she would see him again in some new incarnation. Even now she believed she could feel his presence and lived under his supervision and direction. That was why giving up any of the rules and maxims of her early life was so impossible for her.

She then spoke about her striving to be worthy of her father, who always did "more" and who was seemingly in another world, a world above this one, in which the demands were higher. She felt that people who were born with more gifts should be obliged to give more. "I feel that more is expected of me, and that morally I am obliged to give more. As a matter of fact, I feel that it is something that will absolutely squeeze the last drop that I have to offer out of me, otherwise I have not given enough. Only when absolutely everything has been given, when I really cannot give any more, have I done my duty." She felt this sense of obligation had been important for her anorexic illness: "I was not giving anything to the world, so I did not have the right to eat. I could have a peaceful mind only when I went to bed and couldn't do any more, when I was physically and mentally exhausted. Then I could think, 'Yes, I have a right to sleep and I have a right to eat,' but only then. When I went to bed without being really exhausted and tired, that meant there was still more that I could do and wasn't doing. I was fulfilling my duties by being undernourished and overtired; only then could I feel that I have been doing enough."

She expressed this philosophy in many different ways and over a long time, and she applied it to all activities and relationships. Whenever possible I related these convictions to a child's reaction to the realities of her background; this cruel concept of obligation was a reflection of an upbringing in which she had heard only the demands and expectations that were clearly expressed, but in which she experienced little or no confirmation of her abilities and needs.

As we progressed I formulated more strongly and with many details the unrealistic aspects of this sense of obligation, stating that they represented the world view of a frightened child. Ida admitted that she could see this but was afraid to let go of these obligations: "I'm clinging to them because I don't know what will take their place." My speaking of her undeveloped and unexpressed human qualities was not meaningful to her for a long time. This was exactly what she was afraid of, that her natural self—what she would be if she did not push herself so hard—would not be good enough, that it might be mediocre or even vulgar. I used much of the treatment time to help her become aware of her own gifts, abilities, and contributions, though it took a real sacrifice of pride for her to let go of the superhuman aspirations.

Sara: Hatred and Resentment

Unlike the classic "perfect" family presentation discussed earlier, Sara's family illustrates a more recent type of presentation in which there is open competition and conflict between family members. In this case, as is often the case, the conflict is between mother and daughter.

Sara's mother openly complained about her daughter, a twenty-one-year-old who had been anorexic for five years and in the course of this had developed a bulimia-vomiting syndrome. The symptoms of the illness were so severe that Sara had not been able to stay at college. The only interest she had ever expressed was in becoming an actress, to which her mother was violently opposed. The mother had not hesitated to express her disapproval but emphasized her own frustrated efforts: "She has no respect. She respects her father but not me. She will never listen to me. . . . I gave her dancing lessons, and I had to fight almost all the time to take her there. I gave her piano lessons, and she didn't want that. She fights all the time. She is arrogant and very hostile toward everything I ever try to do for her." Later she added, "I'm afraid of her, and I'll talk to her only when her father is there, because then I know I'm safe."

Sara was just as outspoken in expressing her negative feelings. She admitted that there was a good deal of truth in her mother's complaints. "But there is a lot that she doesn't see about herself. We went to see a lot of psychiatrists, but we always left because when they started saying anything about her she would just leave. She'd say, 'I don't like that doctor—he doesn't know what he's talking about.' "

Sara felt strongly that her mother never had given her a chance to become independent and assume responsibility. "When I was little she used to go through my purse, she used to go through my clothes, she used to clean my room, she used to take me here and there, and she wanted to rule everything I did. She used to be in my whole life. People made fun of her as 'being *my* mother.' She is a bigger neurotic than I am. She has been in my life too much. She has been everywhere—in my life, my whole life. She has taught me that I needed her and that I just can't do without her. When I go off to school, believe me, I do not ever call her and ask her for her help."

The consultation focused on the question of where Sara should be in treatment. She had been at a good psychiatric hospital for about two months, but her parents took her out because she complained about being restricted. Actually the parents had phoned her every day to find out how she was and how she felt, which indicated very strongly that they themselves felt distressed by her absence.

In reviewing her early development, the mother explained the difficulties with Sara in terms of her own life experiences: "See, I was very poor, and I still today scrub the floor and do everything in the house, despite that fact that we could easily afford household help. I am not the type who runs around, and I have tried to instill that in Sara; I wanted her to be the same way." To the question "What did you want to instill in her?" she answered without hesitation, "Humbleness. I wanted her to be kind. I wanted her to study in school. I didn't want to see her drinking. I was never raised that way, and I don't like that kind of living. She would dress up and go to a bar with her friends and wouldn't come home before one o'clock, and I don't like that."

Sara had no hesitation in blaming the illness on her mother: "My mother is the main blame of everything, and I hold this huge hatred for her, I really do. She is very neurotic—if you look at something as a problem it's going to become a problem. Not very long ago I was considered an alcoholic by her because I went out with my friends."

Like so many other anorexics, Sara expressed the wish "All I want is to be left alone, live a normal, healthy life." My response to such statements, and they are very common as declarations of good intent, is something along the lines of "Let's express it in other words: your goal is to be able to lead a normal, healthy life. You haven't lived a normal, healthy life for these past five years, maybe much longer. You have lived an angry, rebellious, resentful, impulsive life." Her response was "Sure. My mother has always told me that I was a problem child. It just infuriates me to think that she was that insensitive to me when I was little. Why couldn't she have seen there was something wrong with me when I was little, or something wrong with her? Why couldn't she see it? How can anyone be that dumb? How could anyone sit there and be that stupid?" My reply was "It isn't quite as simple as that. You could have taken another turn, but this is the turn you took. Don't think I don't appreciate the hardship of your upbringing and that you have tried to take positive steps." Sara replied, "But I have this resentment so bad. I hate even to look at her. That little, naive helplessness—I can't take it. For years and years I wished my parents would get a divorce or something and my mother would have to stand on her own two feet." I explained, "I believe it. Your hatred and resentment is the reason I say that

178

you might not be able to be in treatment on the outside. Your feelings are so strong, and you need human support at the time when you are upset about it." Sara then admitted, "I don't understand this: how come when I get away from Mom, like at school, how come it's the same? How does that have anything to do with my mom, when she was thousands of miles away?" I explained the concept of "incorporation," the fact that Sara's reaction to events that had been upsetting during childhood had become part of her personality. Such feelings no longer depend on the other person being present. "Geography doesn't change a relationship," I told her.

At the end of the consultation, both Sara and her parents were prepared to face the recommendation for treatment at a residential center. In contrast to the previous hospitalization, which had been done more or less on an impulse, they now understood and followed through on the plan.

Carol: A "Good" Family Life

This case dramatically illustrates the contrast between idealized description and repressive action. Carol had lost a considerable amount of weight, from a high of about 150 to a low of 75 pounds since entering college, where she now was a junior. There had been several hospitalizations and consultations, during which the family had been given the impression that they had a "good" family life.

Carol was the oldest child in a successful middle-class family. She described her home in such superior terms that it was difficult to imagine such perfection. It was a place where there were no fights, everyone got along well, and Mother did everything, cooking and taking care of the family. Carol stated, "She helps us. My parents are never domineering." The father stated, "We have a very happy family. I have viewed other people's problems, and in comparison with other people I think we are very happy. I think that Carol felt at one time if she would lose some weight people would like her more. But I don't believe it now."

Carol talked about the meaning of gaining weight: "When you have lost weight for so long and congratulated yourself for every pound you have lost, don't you see how hard it can be to tell yourself that that work was not good?" Her father agreed: "She had so much success at losing weight, and she congratulated herself from being a fatty down to being a skinny. I think weight loss has affected her psychologically. And that's what is worrying us. She can stay the way she weighs now, as long as she is happy with herself and pleased with her life style." I pointed out that it was difficult to imagine a happy life style for someone who was physically so disturbed. The mother added, "The real problem is, she doesn't want to get fat again."

The father assumed responsibility for this, because he had given an example of regaining lost weight. He had been on the rice diet and had lost a considerable amount but had regained it and now was fat again. He asked Carol directly, "Don't you feel proud?" and Carol answered, "I'm not proud that I am this thin. I really am not. I'm embarrassed, kind of." Father interrupted, "But aren't you proud to have control over your weight? Aren't you glad that you did it?" He repeated the question "Aren't you glad?" in several ways.

We reviewed the period during which Carol lost the weight. The mother felt her whole personality changed at that time. "Oh, she was just full of fun, and everybody always said so."

Father introduced, "The whole problem is wanting to please her parents, that's basically the whole thing. And please herself. But our children would do anything to please us. Oh, I think they are the greatest children in the whole world. I really do." And Mother added, "He tells them that every day." Father agreed, "I tell them I love them every single day. I tell them they are the greatest."

I had listened to this exchange and mulled it over. "And now you want to hear something from me? The way you have just interacted is part of the problem. There is a word for this: we call it 'family enmeshment,' where everybody is involved with everybody else. And that happens to be characteristic of anorexic families. The children do not grow up with true independence, self-reliance, and self-direction, and do not feel in control. I have the feeling that Carol's problem is along that line."

Father added, "Maybe she is doing it to please me," to which she responded, "There are other things I could do to please you." He answered, "Everything you do pleases me. You have never done anything that didn't please me." The mother commented, "Well, her daddy has real high ambitions for her—to be a success in life and to be satisfied." When I asked what she meant by high ambition she explained, "He'd like her to be the head of a hospital, or executive dietician for an airline, or something like that." Carol then went into detail about how much she enjoyed her work and studying in home economics. The trouble was that she was always under pressure to have higher grades that would make possible the special education and career that father dreamed of for her.

Previous consultations had overlooked the fact that the father's overambitious plans put enormous pressure on the children and were not compatible with the concept that this was a well-functioning, happy home. It was unreasonable to expect that Carol could make a healthy adjustment as long as she was under this pressure. My chief recommendation was to work with the father (in addition to discussions with Carol) so that he could permit his children greater freedom of development.

Lisa: The "Fraud Girl"

Lisa came for consultation when she was twenty-eight years old, after ten years of anorexic illness. The youngest child by many years, she was born when her parents were well along in middle age. When she was a young child the older siblings were away at school, then they moved away from home, and they were now literally scattered to the four corners of the earth. Lisa had been considered a well-built, somewhat chubby child. At age fifteen, to everybody's satisfaction, she succeeded in bringing her weight down to 115 pounds. At eighteen, during the year she graduated from high school, entered college, and also had a coming-out party, her weight suddenly dropped to 70 pounds.

From then on Lisa vigorously defended her slenderness as her greatest treasure. She considered eating a gross, shameful, and base activity and felt superior to those who indulged their appetites. She finished college with high grades, but her weight on graduation was 59 pounds. Lisa made many efforts, all short-lived, to improve her weight and live independently away from her parents' home. For a while she managed to hold a clerical job, but all other activities were seriously restricted.

Lisa weighed 60 pounds when she came for consultation. She was rather proud that during the past ten years her weight had not risen above 75 pounds. She accepted with much protest the information that nothing valid could be done psychiatrically as long as she was in so severe a state of undernutrition. I outlined a treatment program: she would receive intravenous feeding and, increasingly, solid food to gradually replace the fluid nourishment. Weight gain was much slower than expected, and it became obvious that she manipulated the flow of the alimentation.

Whenever I brought up the need for a more steady increase, Lisa burst out in helpless crying, accusing people of coercing her and making her feel like a failure. She stated that if her treatment was dependent on her gaining weight, she could not do it. It gradually became clear that it was not the food or fatness that she dreaded, but the helplessness she felt to lead the more normal and independent life that would then be expected of her if she were well. She therefore deliberately extended the time of her hospitalization.

About a month after the hospital admission, after her usual angry accusation that nobody understood her split state of mind, she suddenly burst out: "You are correct—I know I would not have needed this if my life had gone differently." She described herself as a happy, normal girl who really did everything the best she could and did everything that was expected of her, but then things went wrong. She still could not understand why things went wrong, but she could see that she had lived a full life that was a fraud. Actually, her whole childhood had not been her own life; rather, she had completely devoted herself to doing what was expected of her. Because her mother had been depressed after Lisa's birth, the father had taken over her upbringing and education. Lisa felt that pleasing him, doing what he expected, was the highest goal of her life. When she felt she no longer could do it, she tried to escape, and having lived a life that she considered a fraud, she developed an illness that was also a fraud. And it was this "fraud girl" who felt she could not eat because then she would have to gain and go back to being Father's obedient servant.

This insight did not change her overall attitude that she wanted to stay thin and refused to weigh more than 75 pounds. We tried to send her to a residential treatment center, but within a month she persuaded her father to take her home. Five years later, after several other unsuccessful treatment efforts had been made, Lisa had been "successful" in her own terms, namely, living at home and maintaining her weight below 75 pounds.

CHAPTER 8

Recovery: Rediscovering the Self

———

THE QUESTIONS of what is involved in recovery from anorexia nervosa—by what signs progress can be evaluated and how far the anorexic condition is accessible to treatment—are complex ones that can be answered from a variety of theoretical viewpoints. Anorexia nervosa is one of the more serious psychiatric conditions, with death or chronic invalidism a not-infrequent outcome. Yet numerous publications speak of high recovery rates in response to certain measures, such as behavior modification and family therapy. I can only deduce that the conflicting observations have been made on widely different patient groups. Best results are reported for very young patients (below sixteen years) in the beginning of their illness, when it has not yet been complicated by contradictory treatment efforts and frightening hospitalizations. Treatment results based on amelioration of the psychological factors, some very subtle, stand in contrast to results based on an exclusive emphasis on the state of nutrition and the return of menstruation. Both factors are necessary for recovery, but if the underlying psychological factors are not clarified the so-called physical improvement usually is short-lived. While it seems that the large-scale reports of remarkable improvement in a short period of time are based nearly exclusively on young patients who appear in a steady stream in clinics with programs that emphasize weight gain as the solution, there is now increasing emphasis on the treatment needs of "older" patients (those sixteen years old or more) and on the need for a comprehensive treatment approach. An essential part of recovery is a change in inner psychological orientation with better reality testing, more trust in being self-directed, and an ability to participate in life with a unified, not split, concept of self and body.

Recovery is not an isolated event that suddenly appears; rather, it is a process that expresses itself in a wide range of subtle changes that occur during treatment. Such changes are reflected most obviously in weight gain and overt behavior changes, but signs of changing attitudes may occur even from the beginning of treatment. The therapist must acknowledge these changes so that the patient can recognize "improvement" in many different areas, such as decrease of muscle tension, more flexible speech, greater interest in people, and a widening range of activities.

Anorexics who were referred to me for consultation for the most part had been anorexic for many years and had been exposed to numerous contradictory treatment plans. Yet they responded amazingly well to a therapeutic approach tuned in to their specific developmental deficits. One of the therapist's early treatment tasks is to recognize how seemingly contradictory attitudes can be brought to a therapeutic and constructive understanding. However, because anorexic patients have rigid thoughts and feelings, it may be quite some time before this understanding can be spelled out to the them. The very fact that there are such discrepancies may be used as a handle to clarify contradictions and help anxious, panicky, and rebellious anorexics to recognize experiences that signal the need for change.

The therapist's task is to focus on the underlying problems that invariably reveal the existence of serious interference in the development of a positive self-concept. It is helpful for the therapist to keep in mind that it is positive and rewarding to help convince someone that she is not bad, empty, and lacking in any positive attributes, as an anorexic usually presents herself. Only reluctantly will an anorexic explore the background of her self-mistrust and self-hatred. The patient begins with defending her solution, namely, skeletonlike thinness and continued starvation, while at the same time expressing guilt and self-accusation for having created so much unhappiness and chaos. Although it takes endless repetition, the therapist's task is to relate these negative attitudes to factual occurrences in the patient's ongoing life situation or against the background of her development. In the beginning there may be a good deal of disagreement between the patient who has kept her mental self-image a deep secret and the therapist who sees this task as helping her to reexamine, or examine for the first time, the faulty assumptions on which her behavior is based. Unless there is a change in the anorexic's basic assumptions about her unending obligations in life, the compulsion to be perfect continues to interfere with her experiencing satisfaction. However, if she makes these changes and her self-doubt gradually diminishes, she can permit her weight to go up.

The examples I presented were intended to illustrate how

deep and far-reaching the changes in the anorexic's self-concept and style of thinking are during treatment. Changes in eating behavior and weight gain have traditionally been cited as signs of improvement—sometimes as the only ones that count. This concept seems to have had a long life in spite of all the evidence that weight gain alone is not a cure, that it is short-lived and may provoke a serious, even suicidal, depression, and that recovery occurs on a much broader basis. I have presented anorexia nervosa here as an effort, a pseudosolution, on the part of the patient to compensate for restrictions of her inadequate early development. A condition such as anorexia nervosa, resulting from complex causes, also involves a complex recovery process. The whole treatment is based on compensating for the deficit in the background; it is an effort to evoke self-reliance, autonomy, decision making, and initiative. Observant and sensitive anorexics are aware of the changes in themselves, and by the end of treatment some can describe in detail how events now affect them differently.

Annette: A New Feeling of Choice

As treatment draws to a close it is important to review what has occurred and what has changed. How this is done depends on the patient's interest in bringing things up. Annette began one of the last sessions by being self-accusing for having nearly succumbed to an old pattern. She was aware that these patterns had happened much more frequently in the past and that she could now step back and look at them in a different way. Yet she was impatient with herself for being tempted by her old tendencies.

Annette had made much overt progress in her years in treatment. Going to an out-of-town college had been very hard, and she took much pride in having been able to stay in Houston on her own, geographically separated from her parents. Over the years she held various jobs, starting as a waitress and proceeding to several positions that were more demanding and befitting her college education. For these she was highly valued for being intelligent, reliable, and conscientious. Although initially she was unable to maintain her weight at the expected level, gradually she began eating normal amounts and maintaining an acceptable weight. She joined several clubs that offered meaningful evening and weekend activities and helped her to overcome her loneliness, though basically she felt isolated for a long time.

Annette's attitude toward achievement and learning became of increasingly practical importance while in treatment because she needed to make a career decision. During her last year in college she had a strong urge to ask her adviser to tell her exactly which profession she should pursue, because she herself did not know. She was aware that this would be inappropriate and therefore did not ask, but she still felt helpless in making a career decision.

She did not make real progress until she had faced several of the basic problems of her development. She had accepted that her great uncertainty and indecision were related to her discouraging childhood experience, of which probably the most damaging was that she could not tell her parents, or anyone else, how she felt. I summarized: "You always held back with the feeling 'I mustn't tell them because it will upset them.' We might define as the real horror of your childhood the fact that you could never honestly complain." She agreed and added, "I was thinking about that yesterday. I was walking across the college campus and thinking how I wished I could start all over again and enjoy the things that were offered to me, given to me, and available. At the time when they were given or offered to me I didn't really want or appreciate those things. It's just so sad."

The following week, again while on the college campus, she had a definite feeling of liberation. While she had been consciously concerned for several years about making a correct professional choice, she was aware that her competitiveness and ambition might steer her in the wrong direction. "Yesterday I wasn't really interested whether I should become a lawyer or historian or get an M.D. or Ph.D. I no longer need a degree to give me content. Now I sort of wonder if I'm after anything at all. I started thinking about other things that might be fun to do—I have even been thinking about teaching."

She felt nostalgic rereading some poems she had read in school. I responded that if she could feel nostalgia, perhaps she remembered now that there had been good experiences as well in her development, that it was not all repressive but there had also been encouragement. She applied this not only to school but also to her home. To other people, her home had looked warm and stimulating. "But I perceived that routine as being inflexible and unchangeable and formal. I believed that it was unspoken but the accepted way of living. I don't think I ever experienced my home as a place of freedom. Later, when I was a teenager, it seemed that all of a sudden everybody changed. That was a confounding experience. I wanted to stick to the rules."

She went into more detail about how she herself had superimposed the rigid rules and how she felt safer by keeping isolated: "The only thing I was trying to do was to feel out which set of rules to follow. The way I felt then, Women's

Liberation or anything like that just went out the window." I commented how often I see anorexics who react in a conforming way to the liberated preaching. "Well, we were susceptible, and if it wasn't that it would have been something else. Women's Liberation provided the opportunity, or said there is opportunity, to do this and be self-respecting. Well, the idea is just looking for another substitution, and because we were living in the seventies the substitution was saying 'Have a career, it's wonderful and marvelous.' We thought we'd been blessed with the something or other. And that's a bunch of hogwash, as far as being the sole motivating force for doing something. I mean, I'm all for Women's Lib saying women should have opportunities and go as far as men and get equal pay for equal work. I get off the boat when they start blaming male society for repressing us, you know. The whole thing of being a housewife is almost a swear word. A lot of it is cultural conditioning."

She continued: "I think I just got a new feeling of choice, a release from an obligation to drive myself to do something that I would perceive as honorable or more than honorable, *extraordinary*. Now I am able to say 'All right, I'll do something that's worthwhile.' Now I'm looking for something that suits my interests. There is no reason to put up with a job or a situation or a city or location or a person that I don't like. I don't have to. There are a whole lot of other things out there. It will take forever, probably, or a lifetime, but I have the confidence that sometime, someplace I'll figure out a place that is suitable for me. I must be suitable to it, and it doesn't have to be a Nobel Prize–winning career."

She went on: "Well, I had a preformed judgment—not looking at myself and my own interests, not looking at my abilities or lack thereof. What a teacher said was good and right, and therefore I must do it, instead of saying 'Well, what do I think?' or 'What do I feel?' I may agree with her or I may not agree with her. But all of a sudden I feel as if the pressure is off, as far as time goes. I had felt I was getting old and gray and had to hurry up and decide what I'm going to do. Now I realize I'll never find out if I don't do something. It was like almost arbitrarily picking something out of a bag and doing it. I may end up in what I pick first or second or third, but I know now it doesn't matter, except that I have to like it."

As in other conditions, the rational recognition of the problem did not immediately translate into action. Considerable working through of many underlying issues was necessary before Annette could take steps to fulfill her self-assertive image and make a successful personal career decision.

Annette came fairly regularly for her appointments, on a three- and later two-times-a-week basis, during the first three years. Once she began professional training the demands of work superseded her interest in treatment, and she came to see me only at irregular intervals, claiming that the appointments conflicted with her work schedule. Early in our work she had been as passive in her attitude toward me as she had been during childhood toward the rule makers. Throughout treatment I stated that I considered it a sign of progress when she could openly disagree with me. With increasing independence she became painfully aware that she continued to be troubled in certain areas by the old childhood attitudes even though intellectually she recognized them as outdated or "antiquated," to use her expression. By the time Annette began professional training, she had developed a better sense of autonomy and would independently think about problems and make observations on her own. She gradually acknowledged that she could see her reactions change.

While she was in active treatment we did much work on "settling" her feelings and attitudes about various family members. Toward the end of treatment it became apparent to Annette, though I had drawn it to her attention many times before, that her relationship to her mother was not "settled." Though loving and friendly, the relationship still existed too much in terms of the old dependency. Annette had clearly recognized as handicapping much of her feeling of being an extra, somebody who must not make demands, of being in the way. When she attempted to discuss this with her mother, as she did several times, her mother reacted to her complaints in factual terms. For example, Annette remembered one family maid as very efficient; in relation to the maid, she felt, "I am just tolerated; a little child must not be in the way." When, while still in therapy, she tried to discuss this with her mother, her mother provided a very favorable description of the maid's reliability and said that she was sure the maid had loved Annette. In therapy we discussed why Annette did not have the courage to tell her mother what she really had experienced. When I challenged her passivity she said, "Well, I recognize what I experienced. And it doesn't make any difference to me if she doesn't know." My reply was "Then you are too modest. I have the feeling it is of great importance to you—I mean from the point of view of the subtle changes one expects—that what you experience is listened to as important, and not as a difference of opinion. For the child, the important thing is that Mother recognizes what is going on in the child." I went on to explain how important it is for a child's development that her feelings are understood and validated: "The question of right and wrong does not enter into this situation. Here we have your mother who does not see how scared you were of her perfect housekeeper." Annette made a conciliatory statement, to which I replied, "Are you completely free of 'I mustn't make any unwarranted demands'?" and she admitted that she was not. "But I know better where it is coming from, and why. I know I have to keep on working on it. But I don't see how it is going to help me or my mother if we go through it again. Maybe at some point it will. But I'm not angry at her anymore for that." I said that it was not a question of anger or justification, but the simple experience that her own reactions were validated and recognized.

To accomplish the difficult changes the patient makes, the same material needs to be gone over again and again in therapy. Through Annette's entire treatment period, I used the episode her parents mentioned during the very first session—that Annette had been patient and friendly and never called when she was through napping—hundreds of times to show that she was too intimidated to express her own needs. I repeated something that had come up quite often: "Being validated in one's own feelings, not changing the attitudes of others, is the important thing. I am sure that I have stated more than once in my thinking about you: the great painful experience, the great unhappiness and suffering of your childhood, was that you had nobody to complain to; and that there was nobody who acknowledged your complaints, your pain, as justified when you experienced them. That is what has been missing and what I still miss in your modesty. There is no intent to convince Mother that she had an inadequate, rigid woman to take care of you. But that under the situation as it worked out, you suffered pain and had nobody to confide in. That is the type of validation that is missing, not only in your life but in the lives of other anorexics too. You are all very well treated, you have the most conscientious homes, most generous homes—the generosity of your parents became a problem for you—but there is nobody to acknowledge your pain and misery."

Annette felt that she should decide whether or when she would have this discussion with her mother, to which I replied, "You are quite correct—it is your decision." She answered, "I guess I just feel that I need to focus my energy now on not repeating what I did when I was four. Some of the overlay, the attitude, the approach is still there, and I've got to work hard not to do it." In reply I tried to correct this: "We are not talking about age four; we are talking about age sixteen, twenty-four, even thirty, when you still feel you aren't fully entitled to the good things in life, when you still feel 'I mustn't make waves.' How did you express it? You feel particularly bad if someone else does something for you that you might have done yourself. You are still restrained in accepting the generosity of others. Or if you accept it, there is still the fear that they consider it an imposition. That's what I am talking about. It started, I think, at age two, three, and four, but it is still active and you still feel horror at my implied suggestions that Mother should share that with you and therefore get tuned in to where you are 'unnecessarily unhappy.'

"What I am talking about is now. What reason do you have to be unhappy? You are a healthy young woman; you are successful in what you pursued; you have the freedom to plan your own future; you can think of yourself as a contributing person, not just socially and professionally but in intimate relationships also. All that is fine. And now comes the big 'But—.' You are no longer that little child who, when they made arrangements for somebody to sit with her during the cocktail parties, felt she was 'in the way, and I mustn't make any demands.' No, I am not talking about age four. I am talking about your making your justified claims on life and feeling slightly guilty both for making the claims and for not being as happy as you are supposed to be."

By this time she had become involved and agreed: "And the fact that the surface looks good, but underneath—nobody suspects." I confirmed this: "Exactly. The tragedy of your life was that under the good surface nobody shared—and you didn't feel you had the freedom, the courage, the confidence to share your unhappiness. I don't want to make it as a concrete suggestion, but think about it as a possibility, that you talk this over with Mother." I made a generalized statement: "It is very easy to reconstruct an unhappy childhood with Father a drunkard and Mother this and that, and a broken home and so on. It is very hard, particularly for well-meaning parents, to understand the unhappiness from the subtle misunderstandings. I believe that it might be of help to you and Mother if you can talk openly about this."

Later in this same session she brought up a few more items. One was, as always, the issue of defining herself through the situations of other people. "I did not want to do anything that would ruffle their feathers. It was particularly in relation to older people that I did not want to ruffle their ways. I had already pegged them as being older, which they were, and very set in their ways. I believed they wanted things just so, and they wanted to be boss. So I was allowing that. And part of that is a rather bizarre idea which had never occurred to me until last week: that as long as I remained a child, then that kept them at the younger age they were when I *was* a child." I repeated what she had said: "Is that what I heard: in a way, by acting like a child you are making time stand still? Since your relationship is fixed, they are fixed and have the privilege of a prolonged usefulness? Do I understand it correctly? Somebody who was sixty when they first knew you as a child, now twenty years later you still define yourself as a child, so they are sixty or sixty-five and not eighty." She confirmed: "And our relationship had never changed such that I felt I could interact with them as anybody but a child."

This fixing the age relationship had come up many times, usually in relation to the summer when she was sixteen and ran the household in her mother's absence. "The age confusion was the essence of everything. When I was a little kid I couldn't be a child. I had to act as if I was this adult; I had to talk to my father about business and finance and something on his level when I was eight years old. Wait a minute—talk about confusion! The bottom line for me, especially with him, was always that nothing of me as a child is valid."

I took this up: "That is the word around which I organized my earlier comments, that what you experienced—the pain and anxiety and criticism—nobody confirmed it as valid for you. But since you used the word yourself, that was what I was talking about. Not that Mother says apologetically, 'If I had known how you felt about the maid, we wouldn't have kept her.' No, that wasn't the goal. But that she recognizes your unhappiness as valid, whereas the nonrecognizing reinforces the unhappiness, and the sharing of it helps to resolve it. But the child who never grows up never gets help on this point."

In the same session I brought up another question: "Thus far we have rediscussed the old problems. My question now is "Are you distant enough from them to recognize or analyze them and to make the step beyond?" She answered, "I'm trying to. None of it comes easily, but since I see it more I can sort of remind myself that I'm stuck in the old dialogue. Someone asks me out to lunch, the automatic response is no. I have to remind myself 'Don't say no, say yes and go,' and I sort of get myself through it. It's still not easy, but I feel as if I'm working on it." I commented, "And the reason why you automatically say no is that repressed childhood feeling 'I am in the way. They don't really mean it. Only Josie expressed the honest truth. She was the mouthpiece and everything else was pretense.' "

Annette herself took up another point, namely, that the feeling of going out to lunch was making her an adolescent, where it all began. "I had this dreadful feeling, 'If I go out to lunch with somebody, what will *they* say? Will my parents approve? No, they won't, so I better not, because I don't want to face the issue with them or him.' " I enlarged: "You believe they felt forced to say yes in order not to appear rigid, but basically you didn't believe that they really wanted you to go. It was so complicated." And she agreed, "It still is. Because all these feelings go around the racetrack once when the issue comes up and then they start all over again. The solution is not to say no and bow to my image of what someone else wants to think, but to go ahead and do what a thirteen-year-old ought to do." I interjected, "Or doesn't want to do, but is curious to try out and find out how she will act in that role." She added, "And is not too keen to be starting where a thirteen-year-old should be when you're twenty-eight." I summarized the conversation: "But it is needed and necessary to be honest about it at twenty-eight, including an honest 'I don't have much experience, so I may feel awkward about certain things, but that's the only way to outgrow them.' It is good that men also vary widely in the way they gain experience with girls and what they expect a girl to be. So there will be men around in the right age and class who aren't the Don Juans everybody wants to appear. It is double-edged. If you are concerned 'How well am I doing?' part of that will be that you expect perfection from the other." Her response was "I know—I am still judgmental. I'm pretty critical, I must say."

I gave a general explanation: "It is very hard to explain things that are so subtle, because what we have come up with aren't overt things that parents did wrong, but a peculiar mixture, always the interplay between a message and the way that message gets handled. And it gets handled in a much more complex way than anybody else ever thought, and the countermessage is misleading. Without understanding this complexity, we would have to assume that everyone in this confusing situation is a liar—which they are not. You remember how intrigued I always was, convinced of the tragedy of the little girl who didn't ask 'Come and pick me up.' I think you have some awareness now what it meant." She enlarged, "They all are, as you say, subtle misperceptions, misinterpretations, everything misses by just a fraction." I responded, "Exactly. It isn't a child who doesn't grasp; it is the opposite, a child who grasps it too well. And what many children do, what we all do throughout life, we all generalize—only you generalized from a little episode like that and devalued all the rest: 'They wouldn't want me to—.'

"What things have you now recognized as important, if not turning points?" She quoted two episodes with the girlfriend who dominated her in the younger grades. One time was when she had taken on a role in a play at the last minute and her girlfriend tore her down for not knowing the lines well enough. Later this same friend reproached Annette for sharing things with her mother. I drew her attention to the important point that Annette generalized from this: "I will not talk to Mother anymore." She explained, "The things I talked to Mummy about, I always thought and still do, were minor. But my friend doubted that I had the judgment to know things. It is as if I was always mad at her so I took it out on myself by not sharing anything." I confirmed this: "That's exactly right. Your exaggeration was 'She tells me I should keep my mouth shut; I'll show her that I can be silent.' " Annette agreed, "Exactly. Looking at myself, I guess the problem was that I was too serious and literal-minded. I didn't allow people to say things that they didn't mean. So when she said 'Don't tell her things,' I didn't fight back by saying 'I know what I can tell her.' "

I confirmed: "Instead of saying, 'I can use my own judgment,' you said, 'All right, I'll show you I can keep my mouth shut.' There is a certain sarcasm in that whole exchange." She agreed, "I am very sarcastic now." And I agreed: "That is the way I have been treated by you. I was one of the grown-ups with whom you didn't quite let it be known how sarcastic you could be." She asked a personal question: "But you detected it anyway?" I acknowledged that I had many examples, but that I did not want to confront her with them because she might experience it as criticism. "But you have become more outspoken about your attitude of 'I can play that game.' I always felt that the bitterness was stronger than the sarcasm in you. The little six- or seven-year-old girl who says at the wedding 'That's how they treat me, like a little box which is forgotten'—that is bitter. The more sarcastic one would have managed to do something embarrassing for them." She agreed, "You are right, it's bitter because I accepted it. It's like everybody had one chance, and if they once blew it, that was it." I added to this, "And to you it meant immediately that it confirmed that your grim view of the world was right."

Shortly thereafter we terminated treatment and she left Houston to pursue her new career. Three years have gone by and from all I hear she is doing well personally and professionally. Not so long ago she wrote in a letter, "I am truly a different person now than ten years ago when I first met you. It's surprising to think so many years have gone by. In one sense, I am younger and more full of life and desire for goals and exploration than ten to fifteen years ago. I hope my ability and opportunities to expand mentally and emotionally can continue in the upcoming years following the lead you initiated."

Ida: The Other Side of the Wall

Ida's weight reached 92 pounds during the second year of her treatment, at Thanksgiving time. A year later her weight was 95 pounds, and the following year it was safely above 100 pounds. It has since stabilized, for over six years, at about 110 pounds, and menstruation has returned. These figures illustrate that for anorexics, regaining the lost weight is often a slow process with ups and downs, a process intertwined with the resolution of the underlying psychological problems.

During the last phase of treatment there is a tendency not only to take stock, to review what has gone on, but also to concentrate on issues that have been neglected or completely overlooked thus far.

Ida showed great interest in her recovery and in reexamining the factors that had contributed to the illness. We also examined what now made it possible for her to look at the illness as a thing of the past. During the last year of therapy we reviewed Ida's whole development and the course of her illness. Repeatedly questions came up concerning the antecedents, what had started it, but also what had kept it going. We focused on two issues. One was the fear of what would happen if she changed. Her fear about the body was closely related to this. She feared that she would blow up, literally, and become obese if she gave up her rigid control over food intake. The other issue concerned her trying too hard to maintain the discipline so that her inner life could not develop. She explained, "But it's not only a façade; it does take discipline. You have the image of yourself, of what you would like to be, and you think you have achieved it. You don't want to give up that image. It would be like a defeat after you have tried to get to this ideal and you are finally there, you think it is wonderful. I always felt that any day I would be on the brink of 'seeing the light.' And when you are constantly feeling something is going to happen any minute, you are hyperaware and tense. You lose your sense of what is normal and you think that the minute you go back to eating 'like a pig,' you lose what you have achieved."

During the recovery phase she spoke with much more spontaneity and honesty about the terrible suffering of this illness, how the hunger experience dominates and changes everything. At the onset of the illness, when she was in Europe, she still enjoyed meals. "I was still uninterested in dieting. I was glad that I had happened to lose some weight, but it wasn't my aim. I still wasn't dieting then. It became an aim somewhere along the time when I started doing a lot of sports. Most of it I enjoyed, but I never enjoyed fencing because it was so difficult. The training was just absolutely exhausting. I was amazed how much my body could take, and I was kind of testing it out. I was amazed that I could go on for days doing three or four hours of sports and about ten hours of studying on two small meals a day, because by that time I had cut out breakfast and ate little. It is so new, you really discover things. It was something that was mine and I was doing it. Nobody in my family was doing fencing and no one was doing it as well." She took fencing nearly as an eccentricity. "The more eccentric I was considered, and when people told me I was crazy, I was flattered! They couldn't have told me anything more flattering in the world." Pursuit of thinness became a goal in itself and she did not want to give up what she had accomplished. "I was convinced that I would explode if I gave in and ate. You are so delighted that you can do it that you lose track of everything else."

She recalled her problems with sleeplessness, hyperacuity, and loss of the sense of time. "All I knew was whether it was day or night. There was a certain structure in being driven to school—just being moved from home to school and back to home. Eating was something you avoided—somehow you just did it when it was forced on you. You are in a constant daze— you do not feel as though you are really there. It came to the point that I doubted the people around me; I was unsure whether they truly existed. I no longer could communicate with people—there was really nothing to talk about, and there was this constant feeling that they wouldn't understand anyhow."

Her experience of time was confusing, alternating between terrible acceleration and such slowness that the days were endlessly long. She slept only three hours, staying awake and doing something for the remaining twenty-one hours. "Time might go very fast—but then came the feeling that time had stopped altogether, or that it was irrelevant. It was strange. If I say 'now' I mean this minute, or something that I am doing right now, here. But in that extreme other state the concept of time, of the here and now, was gone. It was all unreal—I don't quite understand it and can no longer explain it. I was proceeding as if time just did not exist. There was day and night and that was all. During the day there was a whole lot more light that was painful and I couldn't enjoy it, and a whole lot more busy activities and people who demanded things, and there was no calm. I was happier at night. That's why I stayed up so late and refused to go to bed. At night there was silence and it was cool. If there had not been day and night I really would have forgotten everything and would not have had a sense of existence."

One of the things that kept her going was the extraordinary pleasure she derived when she permitted herself some indulgence. "I find it impossible to describe the pleasure I would get out of a cup of coffee which I permitted myself late at night, when I had the lights dim. It was warm and made me feel better because I felt cold—the pleasure was so great that it is indescribable in words; it was like real ecstasy. Now I would say that it is no wonder that when you are starving and cold a cup of coffee is delightful."

She used an interesting image to describe this period of her life: "You create an artificial wall between you and the rest of the world. The trouble is that it is so hard to break. It should have been broken down before the mortar got fixed, and now that it is fixed I kick against it and it won't budge." I agreed with her that this image described it well: "You erect kind of a temporary wall, but instead of staying loose it gets mortarized and becomes indestructible."

She also recalled the continual struggle with school work, when writing reports was a tremendous effort: "The whole life is like you are carrying a cross—something heroic, something that is very difficult and demands admiration. I felt doing something that was not hard was quite inconceivable; it would be lazy and despicable. Life was like the labors of Hercules—things he was forced to do though he didn't like them. That's what I felt life was—everything was a heavy duty thrown onto me." Little if any of this had been expressed directly during the state of acute starvation, though it was recognizable in the defensive irritability when I attempted to understand the meaning of her behavior.

In another session she talked about the early dieting: "I can laugh now at what I used to do. But I am having difficulty recalling details. I was searching to find exactly what I was supposed to do, what I was here for. I felt that the way to get at it was through all this chastising yourself, being very disciplined, in a sense being 'perfect.' But that has changed now. An interesting example is what I have noticed in the difference in my swimming. When I first came I used to go swimming during lunchtime to avoid eating. Now I go three times a week during lunchtime, but there is a whole world of difference because afterward I go and eat."

At one time she was mildly upset and feared that she might not have completely outgrown her anorexic preoccupations. She had suddenly felt alarmed about having eaten too much of a tasty casserole, and the old question "How much more can I gain?" troubled her again. She explained it as it related to her concern about a friend at college, who had gone on a very rigid diet and who Ida feared might develop anorexia. "I know exactly how she feels; I see her strained face and hear her say that she is not hungry, that she does not need to eat. I know what she is undergoing. I see her spending hours on her assignments. I know she cannot concentrate, and that however hard she tries she keeps on thinking about food, and that is why it takes her hours to finish her work. I suffered through it myself."

But now it was inconceivable to Ida that she had expected to change her role in the world by going hungry, by trying to fulfill superhuman obligations. She felt the first breakthrough had come when she began eating here and snacking there, and realized, "It isn't all that terrible. The smallest things were the greatest luxuries. Then came a long period of wondering how do other people do it, how come not everybody is fat. And then I noticed that some people would procrastinate and not do things immediately.

"Then came the next period, and that was when I was really getting better and the real switch came, when I got out of the cage, when I began starting to enjoy life a little bit more and sharing more with others. It had started with feeling, 'You just don't care about people, whether they approve or how they do it.' I realized people are just the way they are, that is their thing and I'm here and I do it my way. Then I started thinking that people were fascinating, and only then did I become interested in people. Until that time I had paid attention to people to compare myself but not as truly interested. When I first got interested in men the talk was still about theater and politics, but then it was all uphill. It is difficult now for me to envision the total self-absorption before that. I must have been awfully obnoxious at that time. I recall girls saying toward the end of my second year 'It was only in these last few months that we have come to know you.' I only had polite intercourse, 'good mornings' and 'good nights.' I really was like a shadow; I don't know why, but it sure was strange."

She recalled the summer after her freshman year, when she had traveled in Europe with a small group of students but had never felt close to anyone: "The richness of my life consisted at that time of ideas, not of concrete things, certainly not of people. I had made a point of being 'independent' of the world, so to speak." She recognized now that severe isolation and true independence are not the same.

"In a sense I was not prepared for what I realize now, that the richness of the world is the attraction of people. Ideas are nice, but they are not substantial. Somehow I must have felt,

'They are mine, you can't take them away from me.' Only slowly did I begin to realize that you do have things in common with people, that you feel certain things. I had felt cut out of that so I felt if my life is going in a different way, well, I just have to go in a different way. I thought at that time that our work here involved my having to start being able to have these relationships with people on a more human, emotional level. But I was not going to give up everything else on account of that. In comparison to that I definitely think now that people are important. I like having companionship. I like going to classes because it is something more alive than to read a book on your own. Formerly it wasn't that I didn't want to make friends, but I felt that everyone was very interested in what they were doing and so was I. In a way friendship to me was like a common isolation. I really couldn't conceive of a friendship that would be involved with trivia, just having fun together. I couldn't conceive of procrastinating. Literally, talking to people was wasting time. Now I do a lot of talking and I do not consider it a waste of time."

In reviewing the development of her illness, Ida felt it started quite some time before the weight loss began. "I started my tremendous questioning everything and being very, very confused. I can't tell what I was confused about, but it was also related to the death of my father. It helped confuse me more. It is interesting to me when I am talking with friends now, reading poetry and so on, to find out that they had also been confused. What was damaging in my case was that I didn't communicate this confusion to anyone else. My brother didn't take an interest in it." She felt the only person she had communicated with was her father, and in a way she had kept him alive and still could communicate with him.

We examined the steps toward recovery in many discus-

sions. Ida recalled, "Well, the first step I took was the willingness to be curious, to see 'how could it be different.' That was
in fact the period when I still was very condescending in many
ways. But with all my condescension I realized that there is
more to life: 'Well, I will go along with it for a while and find
out what it is all about.' That was my attitude when I first came
here. I kept feeling it was sort of funny because I was very split
in my thinking. On the one hand I felt I would observe myself
change, and on the other it suddenly dawned on me—it was
the period of the crisis about losing too much weight—I guess
that I could not watch myself change and not change. It was
much more complex than that. I realized I couldn't play-act
forever. I used to think, 'Oh, I can always get by with compro-
mising.' Then I became panicky because I realized I couldn't
compromise forever. Something had to be shown. So I gained
a little bit of weight, then I would lose it and gain a little bit.
The thing about just how much I could weigh was 'what was
the minimum I could buy to get the psychological treatment.'
Because I've got to do a lot of talking, and I had never talked
to anyone before, and that was nice and I wanted to continue
with that."

She was indefinite when I asked her when the change had
occurred: moving beyond superficial agreement that covered
the quiet thought "But I know better, it isn't so." "Somewhere
along the line—I don't know how it happened. But I realized
that I had to do something, I couldn't just sit there and wait
for things to happen. I realized I had missed out on this so I
needed a better start. At times I got panicky that I wasn't going
to change, or that I was missing or had missed a lot of things
that I hadn't given importance to and now I recognized that
they were important. There was a long time when being skinny
was all-important. Things changed when I discovered how nice

it was to be with people, to talk with people or to discover that they didn't think I was stupid or uninteresting."

In this context she expressed genuine gratitude toward her mother for having recognized that she was ill and doing something about it: "She called you. She did everything at that time. I kind of went along with it but didn't realize it."

During the last phase of treatment she felt safe from relapse into anorexic behavior but still had periods of self-doubt, of feeling empty or being bothered by the question "Who am I?" The fear of her not being good enough if she would let go reappeared in many different forms, now no longer as overwhelming doubt but as something capable of reassessment. She could recognize that as long as she was anxious about not being good enough, she would cling to some unrealistic goal. She admitted that each new step forward aroused the old fear of being deceived, the way she had always felt deceived in her family where nobody paid attention to her when she was miserable. "I felt right along that I was leading a fake life, to cover up the fear of failing." She recognized this self-devaluation as the essence of the illness, of which she could free herself only by accepting her genuine self, undeveloped though it might be, as good enough for her. Toward the end of treatment she expressed it as "You give what you have to give and not what you don't have."

In spite of the pain and suffering that the anorexia had caused, she felt that it had played a positive role in her life, that without it she might have been stuck with her overdependent attitude toward her family. The other positive aspect was that it led to therapy, which helped her develop true independence and self-respect. When she was asked about the old image of the sparrow in a golden cage, she explained that the idea of having been caged was still with her but she felt that she herself

209

had created the cage. "Once you set a pattern for yourself you want to live up to what you think everybody is expecting from you. It is this artificial pattern that becomes a cage, something to impress people." She felt that treatment had helped her to break down the cage, and she had outgrown the ideas that had built it.

Index